So You Want to Date My Daughter?!!!

A Program for Dating with Destiny in Mind

Joel and Linda Budd

CrossStaff Publishing

So You Want to Date My Daughter?!!!
Dating With Destiny in Mind
ISBN 978-0-9800755-1-9
Copyright © 2008 by Joel and Linda Budd
1439 East 71st Street
Tulsa, OK 74136

Dedication

To our three lovely daughters,
who have become three lovely brides:

Cristin Budd Hamman

Joelle Budd Burris

Haley Budd Cone

And to their three godly husbands,
who have become our sons:

Shane Hamman

David Burris

Chris Cone

Acknowledgements

When it comes to love and dating, there is only one perfect example for us on how to romance and win a bride ... that's Jesus Christ. What a lover! Unquestionably, Jesus is wildly passionate and His heart is filled with extravagant, fiery love. Yet, He is always pure and humble in His pursuit of a bride. That's the model we are going for.

Jesus is the source of any truth found in these pages. Any mistakes are all ours.

We feel so rich and grateful for the opportunities we have been given over the years to help friends and families in their dating adventures. We have been given a great honor to have been invited into the lives of some very precious people, and to help coach them in their dating seasons. The love and encouragement these couples have given us has helped make us willing to put this dating outline in print so others can take a glimpse at what has worked for us and perhaps give it a try.

Scott Kaste and CrossStaff Publishing have once again been an incredible gift to us in providing much needed counsel, encouragement, motivation and selfless support.

Table of Contents

Foreword

At the age of twenty-three years I was living a fast-paced, California lifestyle, sleeping with three girls regularly, and was essentially engaged to be married to two of them. As one who had attended church on most weekends for most of my life, I should have been the poster-boy of chaste living. But as far as I knew, Christianity had nothing practical to say about dating. It certainly couldn't teach a guy how to stay sexually pure in his romantic relationships.

God was about to change my opinion on that score.

I'd been riding hard at work for months, striving to make my mark in the business world, and the pace on one particular day in May had been no exception. I'd been pushing all day long, skipping dinner and making phone calls well into the evening. By now it was late and everyone else had gone home.

I was beat, so I decided to call it a wrap. As I straightened up my desk, I casually glanced out my west window and was stopped in my tracks. Unfolding before my eyes was an unbelievably grand California sunset. As a reward to myself for a long day of work, I decided to kick back in my chair and take it all in before locking up and heading home.

Lacing my fingers behind my head and propping my feet on the credenza under the window, I leaned back in my chair with a satisfied sigh. Life was good. But just then this pleasant scene was shattered by an intruder ... the Lord Himself. He interrupted my world, breaking into the moment to contrast that indescribably beautiful sunset with my hopelessly ugly life, especially my relationships with women. My satisfied sigh turned to sorrow and despair, and tears began streaming down my face. The picture of my life was so awful that even today my eyes well up whenever I think back on it.

Seeing my life through Jesus' eyes, I really had no choice about my next move. Immediately I turned and reversed the course I'd been on, praying: "Lord, I'm ready to work with You if You're ready to work with me." I stood up and walked out of the office, not yet fully realizing what I'd just done. But God knew, and it seemed as if all of heaven began to move in my life. Within a few weeks I had a job back home in Iowa and a new life ahead of me. I'd left the girlfriends, and the sin, far behind. My life has never been the same since.

My thinking also has never been the same since those early days, which has a lot to do with Joel and Linda Budd. Soon after landing back in the Midwest, I strolled through the doors of a central Iowa church where Joel and Linda were serving as young, twenty-something associate pastors. It was Sunday school hour, and I hadn't a clue where to go. As my finger trailed down the list of opportunities available to me that morning, my eyes kept bouncing back up the list to Joel and Linda's marriage class.

Why? I didn't have a wife. In fact, I didn't even have a girlfriend. But I did still have that horribly fresh, sunset view of my ugly, hopeless lifestyle sitting on my mind. I knew if there was anything in the world I needed to learn, it was how to treat women right.

For the first time in my life I felt completely lost when it came to women. Because of my own selfishness and sexual sin, it seemed as if everything I knew about them came from one-night stands and casual dating relationships, and that simply wasn't enough anymore. While I hadn't yet sworn off dating completely, I knew I wasn't the least bit ready to date again. I wasn't at all sure I could even spot the right kind of girl for me.

I wandered on down to Joel and Linda's class and settled nervously into my place as the only single man in the group. That wasn't easy for me, and it wouldn't surprise me a bit if I am still the only man in history to have attended a married couples' class for a whole year without even having so much as a single date! But I'm glad I did it.

I was completely mesmerized by the practical, "how-does-scripture-look-in-real-life" teaching style from that first day, and then forward. I remember how Joel began to lay out the glorious differences between men and women. He taught me how those differences complement one another in a romantic relationship, and how we, as men, need to adjust our thinking and act accordingly.

Like a master artist, Joel's words also painted the bright, swirling inner beauty of women and the glory that God intended them to carry into our lives as couples. It was amazing. After all the time I'd spent with women, I was appalled at how little I knew about them and was awed by the potential impact a woman's inner nature might have upon a man's life.

It wasn't long before I just had to see one of those awesome, lovely creatures. So just before the nine-month mark in the class, I prayed this simple prayer: "Lord, I've learned a lot about women, but I'm not sure I've ever seen or really known any Christian girls. Please show me a woman who embodies godly characteristics." I wasn't asking for a date, a girlfriend, or a spouse. I just wanted to see the teaching in practice, in real life, so I might understand even better.

In the end, God did far more than that for me. One week later He introduced me to my future wife, Brenda, and we fell in love. It was awesome. God Himself arranged our marriage, but the biggest miracle was that I could even pray that prayer in the first place. I had gone from being unsure of my ability to spot the right kind of girl for me to being absolutely certain I could spot one if God would just bring one around. The teaching in Joel and Linda's class had been so practical and true that even a baby Christian could understand how it should all look and play out.

Obviously, I'd been wrong about Christianity, hadn't I? God does have practical things to say about dating. And the best part about the Lord is that when you ask Him to teach you something, He will. He loves you. He is your Father, and He wants to teach you all the things that work, in practice. He wants you to live an abundant life on this earth.

When it comes to God's willingness to answer us in practical ways, no one understands that any better than the Budds, who have always been focused on the practical side of things, especially when teaching their own daughters. In fact, if you fast forward twelve years or so from the story I just shared, you'll find the Budds asking God a question about their girls and dating that was very similar to mine: "Lord, how can I help my daughters sort out the good from the bad when dating? How can I help them to have fun while dating without being damaged in the process?"

Joel and Linda knew God would answer them, and He did, blessing them with some of the most simple and practical biblical teaching on healthy dating I've ever encountered. Happily, you are about to encounter that same blessing. But before I turn you over to the Budds, it's critical to ask you a very important question in preparation: Do you really think it's possible to date purely in this day and age? Sure, we all know how we're supposed to answer that question, but that's not what I want from you. I want the truth. What do you really believe is possible these days?

Many Christians don't believe it is possible to date purely anymore, except by luck or by some fortunate set of circumstances. In a culture as dark as ours, it's simply not possible to teach the scriptural truths in such a way that we can really count on the results. Bob is one of those Christians. I ran into my old friend one Saturday morning and recalled how we'd shared some happy conversations about his grandchildren over the past couple of years. That reminded me of some exciting news that I was certain he'd appreciate.

"Hey, Bob!" I called, my eyes twinkling. "Do you still have some room for me in that special little club of yours?"

Arching his eyebrows, he looked puzzled. "What club is that, Fred?"

"You know, the grandparent's club! We are due to have our first!"

"That's fantastic, Fred!" Bob smiled brightly. "Who's having the baby?"

Clunk! Now it was my turn to be puzzled. Bob knew my four kids very well, and he also knew that only my first-born, Jasen, was married. What kind of a question is that? I thought.

"Jasen and Rose, of course," I finally stammered. "He's the only one who's married, remember?"

"Well, you know how it is these days with dating, Fred. You never know if you don't ask," he replied casually.

I was incredulous. "Sure you can know, Bob. We aren't just talking about anybody here. We're talking about the Stoekers!" I said with a grin, thinking, We're Christians, remember? You can teach teens God's ways. They can stand. You can count on the results.

Not in his mind. My response didn't click for him. Shrugging his shoulders, he congratulated me once more and headed for his car, but I grieved for two days. We'd sat together in the same church for over twenty years and we'd heard the same teachings together again and again, and yet this blessed man of God didn't believe that the practical truths of Scripture can keep kids chaste out there in the real world of dating. To him, it's a given: Most young people will fall to sexual sin, and since Christianity can't change that, you certainly can't count on having all your grandkids come from your married children.

Is that what you believe?

I don't. You see, it doesn't matter what "these days" are like out there. What matters is whether you have God's truths on purity and dating painted so practically into your life that you can't miss the Father's heart and you can't imagine violating His boundaries on the matter.

Joel and Linda have laid out God's truths to me many times over the years, but it's always been their practical side that has jarred me the most, and it's been no different on the topic of dating. If you don't believe pure dating is possible, Joel and Linda are about to jolt your senses back in line with God's ways, through some very practical teaching. Read what they have to say. Apply the truths, and take them on as your own.

It's time to believe again, my friend.

If you're the one out there dating, you can stand purely. You can stop promiscuity in its tracks, and you can keep roving hands at bay — all the way to the altar. In fact, if you approach dating this practically, it's not only possible, it's extremely likely.

If you're a parent, you can teach your kids to walk purely, no matter how putrid the culture. Pure children are not just the luck of the draw. You can teach them truths so practical, and indelible, and strong that they'll be able to stand purely, even beneath the emotionally white-hot spotlights of dating. You have a say in it. You can help them. It's true.

God's ways are as protective and powerful in the dating arena as they are anywhere else. Ask your Father to teach you what you need to know as you read this book. He will.

Fred Stoeker
Author of *Every Man's Battle"* and *"Hero"*

Introduction

Joel and Linda: When we originally delivered this teaching to our church family some years ago, we were stunned by the overwhelming response. We had no idea how hungry and desperate people were for a scriptural, practical approach to dating. Since that time tapes and CDs of that message have traveled all over the world, and year after year it continues to be one of the most frequently requested messages from our bookstore.

Many people have urged us to get the message in print because the resulting testimonies are amazing. So we have put some testimonies of young adults who have used this dating outline (Chapter 16) at the back of the book. They will really encourage you! We meet dads who tell us, "I didn't have a clue how I was going to guide my daughter through this dating thing. I got a copy of your message and took notes. Now I'm using your outline and it has taken much of the fear and helplessness out of it all." Another comment we hear often is, "My daughter and I are closer than we have ever been. I feel like I'm a key player in her dating life, and we both like it. In fact, it's kind of fun!"

Although this book describes how we guided our daughters as they dated, became engaged, and were married, we know from so many others that you can be creative in adapting the information to your dating season, or to your family. You may not have daughters - you may have sons, or perhaps both sons and daughters. You may even be a single parent. For these reasons, we are not only giving you our dating outline, but are also giving you a foundation from God's Word.

Today we personally do not do any counseling, except in very special circumstances, because it is not what God has called us to do, but we made it a priority to develop a great counseling department in the church that handles any counseling need for our people. However, in the past when we did counsel young men and women who wanted help with dating, we used the principles in this book to guide them. We also used this outline with young couples who were engaged to be married, as well as parents and teenagers who were trying to navigate their way through the dating scene. We know these principles can work for every family!

We encourage you to study and meditate on God's Word regarding the issue of dating, courtship, and marriage. Pray about the guidelines and procedures we recommend in this book and seek the Lord's wisdom in adapting them to your family and situation. Whether you have sons or are a single parent, you will be able to use these principles to create your own dating outline and your own ways of guiding your children as they go through the exciting process of growing up, dating, and finding the mate God has for them. If you are an unmarried young adult who wants direction and confirmation about Christ-centered dating, this outline will definitely help you grow and become the right person as you watch and wait for the right person God has for you. And when you find someone you wish to date, this outline will be of great help if you want Christ in the center of your dating adventure.

Using this book as a guide, and knowing that you are standing on God's Word and being led by His Spirit, we believe you will have new faith and hope. You will find that the teenage and young-adult years do not have to be the nightmare the world says they are. If you are a parent, please know that you can actually enjoy the process of helping your children handle dating relationships God's way. Like us, as your children marry, you will be overjoyed at the great people they choose to bring into your family.

As a believer, God wants you to enjoy every aspect of the lives of your family members. And He wants to be a part of everything because He is your Father! He is your Heavenly Daddy! So we encourage you to allow Him and His Word to guide you as you guide your kids — just like He has us. We promise you this: Our Father is the most awesome dating and relationship coach you and your family will ever know!

Chapter 1

A Bad Boy Becomes God's Man

Joel: When I was seventeen years old I had already lost my virginity and was living promiscuously. I didn't mean to be a bad boy, I just drifted into it. I had been dating the way most kids today date: without a plan or purpose. I was relating to the opposite sex with no sense of destiny or direction - it was all about whatever I wanted and needed in the moment.

In my family, if you lived at home then you went to church. Since I wasn't ready to go out on my own, every Sunday I was in church, but I wasn't happy about it. I had long hair and dressed sloppy. I would sit at the back of the sanctuary, slouched down, my feet on the chair in front of me, usually reading a secular book to keep me occupied through the service. I was a poster child for rebellion.

Once in a while I showed up at youth camps my church attended. At one particular youth camp, I remember clearly how my pastor sat down beside me, looked at me, shook his head, and said, "You know, Joel, I really don't think there is any hope for you." Just to make sure I heard him he shook his head again in frustration and said, "In all my years of ministry I've never said this about anyone, but I really don't think there is any hope for you."

Frankly, to me his words were just another example of another typical adult who didn't know me, didn't care to know me, and just didn't care.

Communication was not a real strength in my family. My parents never asked me what I wanted to do with my life, much less if I had given my life to Jesus. It was an unaffectionate atmosphere where we rarely communicated with one another, so it was easy for me to think, Since there's no hope for me, I might as well do what I feel like doing. I continued to drift through life, just getting by and acting on impulse.

Then, during one Sunday night service, the pastor got my attention when he introduced Linda.

Linda Rocks My World

Stunned, I looked up from my book to see who the pastor was bringing up to testify and saw a very attractive girl. I was suddenly curious to find out who she was and hear what she had to say, so I actually paid attention for once in a church service.

Linda blew my mind. She was a little younger than me and had just gotten saved. Unlike me, however, she talked about coming from a completely pagan home - they never went to church or talked about God. But similarly, her home was completely dysfunctional. She talked about how Jesus had come into her heart and saved her, how He had given her a brand-new life; and how her heart was completely changed. I had never heard, much less seen, anything like what she was describing before.

I was stunned. This girl's heart was fresh and tender. I thought, she is genuine, and she's a knock-out to look at! I remember realizing that more than anything else that stood out to me, she really seemed to know Jesus in a personal way. She talked about

Him like He was her best friend instead of some religious figure who lived a long time ago and was hardly relevant in our world today. To her, He was real and wonderful. To her, God was not some angry judge who couldn't wait to punish her every time she made a mistake.

When the pastor had Linda get up to speak on Sunday evenings, which he often did, I dismissed whatever book I was reading – I was incredibly attracted to her, and she always got my full attention! Yet in reality, I was provoked by her faith and her unusual relationship with the Lord. I was confronted by the fact that she had something I didn't have — a sincere, intimate relationship with a trusted friend, Jesus.

From even that first Sunday night when she gave her testimony, I hoped that somehow she was attracted to me, but I was too scared to find out. She was not the kind of girl I was used to dealing with.

Every now and then I would go to our church's coffee house downtown. It was an outreach to teenagers and young adults, and I was fully aware of the possibility that Linda just might be there.

On one particular night, I decided to leave my car at the coffee house and catch a ride with a friend, who was a pothead and was really wild. We drove around town for a while before driving back to the coffee house. As he stopped the car, he saw Linda walking into the coffee house. "Wow!" he cried. Then he whistled at her and called out, "Hey, would you go out with me?"

Linda turned around just as I was getting out of my friend's car, but thought I was the one who had just yelled to her! She came right over to me. At that moment I had just enough brain activity to remember that my high school's homecoming football game the next weekend was against her high school. I knew she was a cheerleader and would be at the game.

I managed to squeak out, "Hi," before I quickly cleared my throat and went on, "Uh, I have to be at the homecoming thing at half-time, when your school is playing my school, so how about if I meet you at the game?" I was too afraid to really ask her out, but, to my surprise, she said she would meet me there!

When the night of the homecoming game arrived, all I could think about was seeing Linda. After I had participated in the homecoming activities at half-time, I went over to her and asked her if I could give her a ride home. I forgot that because she was with the visiting school and had ridden to the game in a bus with the other cheerleaders, she had to have written permission from her parents to ride home with someone else, but to my amazement, she not only said, "Okay," but she took out a permission slip from her parents saying that I could take her home! Even then, I did my best to make the opportunity not appear as a date - I was still afraid she would reject me.

As I drove Linda home that fall evening, I started asking her questions about her relationship with God. Even though I knew all the right answers, because I'd been hearing them all my life, I needed to hear them from someone who was really experiencing something I had only half-way heard preached on Sundays. I had the right theological answers in my head, but no real relationship with

God in my heart. It was a long-ago, far-away memory to me, but it seemed so real to her that it drew me in with curiosity. Her tenderness and vulnerability to Jesus was melting the super-structure of my rebellion.

My mother must have noticed my attraction to Linda because right after my homecoming game she invited her to my birthday party. It was at my party that I did what I tell every young man and woman not to do - I gave into my feelings and expressed them before we had even gotten to know one another. As soon as I had an opportunity, I took Linda aside, I blurted out, "I'm absolutely in love with you but I don't want to get hurt. I don't know if you have any feelings for me, but if you don't, then please tell me now."

She replied, "I feel very strongly for you too."

The Holy Spirit Finally Has His Way

The following Sunday, and from that time on, I sat with Linda toward the front of the church. We would hold hands, and I began to pay attention to the sermons like I had never done so before. Through the worship and every sermon that was preached, I was hearing and seeing the Gospel through her eyes - it was all different to me. From that time on, whenever we went on dates, our conversation would always turn to the things of God.

My family never said a word to me about dating Linda, but the pastor had plenty to say to Linda! When he heard she had started dating me, he became deeply upset because Linda was such a special young woman of God. She would get up in church and give her testimony whenever asked, and the people always responded to her. Furthermore, she was leading many of her classmates, friends, and family to the Lord.

One night at church the pastor took Linda aside and said, "I heard you are dating that Joel Budd." When she confirmed the report, he said, "Oh no," shaking his head as he walked away. Linda was very confused because of what God had told her. When she had first seen me, sitting in the congregation with a rebellious, I-don't-care attitude, the Lord had told her, "That's the man you're going to marry. You're both going to be pastors, and you're going to have three children." Being Linda, she just accepted what the Lord said with child-like faith and continued to see me, even after our pastor had confused her with his response.

Then, on one particular Sunday night, the Holy Spirit got to me too. That evening, as I went to the altar and surrendered my whole life to God, He immediately began speaking to me about my future. He not only told me that I was to go to Bible college, He told me I was to go to a specific Bible college, even though I had never stepped foot on the campus or made any inquiries about it. This college had never even crossed my mind!

When I finally went back to my seat, I told Linda what God had said about Bible college. To my surprise, she said, "I already knew that!" To me, it was a miracle that the girl I loved also loved me, but I finally realized she was an incredible gift from God.

Unfortunately, when we had first met, I did not see her as a precious gift. I was drifting and self-centered, like the prodigal son who ate with the pigs in the mud. All I wanted was to please myself, but the Holy Spirit had changed my heart at the altar that night. For the first time, I began to see her the way He saw her, and it really humbled me.

The Holy Spirit began to take me through a wonderful, effective restoration process. As I repented and confessed my sins, the Lord Jesus forgave me, and when I confessed all of my past sins to Linda, she forgave me also. The Lord Jesus restored a precious purity to my life that I treasured, just as I also treasured the precious purity and gift of Linda.

The Plan

Linda and I continued to date, but since I had graduated from high school, I moved to Des Moines, Iowa in the fall to attend Bible college. Like a love-sick puppy, I still called her every day and drove five-and-a-half hours each way every other weekend to see her. Because the drive was so long that we didn't have much time together, but still wanted to be together at every available opportunity, I came home with a ring that Christmas and were engaged.

A few months later I realized I had not gone about the engagement the proper way, so I went to her dad and apologized for not asking for his blessing before proposing to his daughter. His response was simply, "Yeah, that's all right. If I have to have a son-in-law it might as well be you!"

A new plan was quickly formulated: when Linda graduated from high school in the spring, she would move to Des Moines, get a job, and we would get married the following fall; however, by the time she graduated and had been living in her new apartment in Des Moines for a couple of weeks, we both realized that plan was just not going to work. One afternoon, I blurted out, "I don't want to wait a year! You're lonely living by yourself, and I'm sick of living with a bunch of smelly guys in the dorm. What do you say we forget the big wedding and elope?"

Linda immediately said yes, but the excitement was short-lived as we realized she was too young to sign the marriage license. (At that time, you had to be twenty-one and she was just eighteen.) She needed her parents' written permission in order for our marriage to be legal.

I called her father and said what any unthinking, crazy-in-love young man would say, "I know we said we would marry in a year, but we just can't wait. We want to be together now. I know you don't want us to move in together - you want us to do this right, so we want to get married this weekend, but we need your permission because Linda's not twenty-one. Would you possibly sign the papers if we send them to you, so we can elope?"

Thankfully, her father agreed. Shortly after, a local pastor gave us one hour of pre-marital counseling and then married us, but, of course, it was not the "happily ever after" ending we thought it would be.

Reality Sets In

Linda and I were totally in love with each other, but both of us had come from dysfunctional families which had a lot of emotional wounds and relational issues. We had no idea how to communicate with each other or discuss problems. To make matters worse, we were both so wounded and insecure from our growing-up years that we continually hurt and offended each other without knowing how or why.

Despite our personal problems, I graduated from Bible College and we became pastors just as the Holy Spirit had told us. Just a few years later, we began to grow our family with the three kids God had told Linda we would have. While we loved each other deeply and were totally committed to our marriage, we suffered in our relationship until neither one of us could accept the way we were any more. After ten years, we finally went for marriage counseling.

Our first counselor was a disaster and we gave up on counseling for another few years. Eventually, however, the Holy Spirit gave Linda the name of a counselor as she was crying out to God about our marriage - the Lord spoke the name of a certain individual to her mind. She had never heard of him before, but when she checked into it she found, to our amazement, that she had correctly heard the name of a real counselor in that area. The miracle of that "coincidence" renewed our hope and we purposed to try again.

Gratefully, our second counselor was wonderful! He taught us communication skills and we began to discuss our issues without continually hurting and offending each other. Later, we went through the process of personal revival and discovering the Father's love that we describe in detail in our books, Fill Me or Kill Me and No Longer Bound.

I urge you to read these books if you want to know how the Holy Spirit can take two completely dysfunctional believers and begin to heal their hearts and set them free from all their past wounds, rejection, and insecurities. You name it and He has amazingly healed it in us! As grateful as we were for counseling, no amount of it could have accomplished for our hearts what began to happen in us as we experienced the accelerated healing power of the Father's love.

Looking back over our relationship, what I know now is that God used Linda in a powerful way to bring me to Himself. Every time I wake up in the morning and see her shining face, I am reminded that she was the motivation that caused me to turn from being a bad boy. She was my first inspiration to become a strong and loving man of God. And in all honesty I can say that I am more in love with her today and more attracted to her heart now than I was thirty-five years ago. For all these things I am eternally grateful.

Looking to the Future

What Linda and I went through in our dating years, short engagement, spontaneous wedding, and then our marriage, became our inspiration to train up and guide our three daughters in God's ways so that they would not have to go through the difficult, and often heart-breaking times, we had gone through. When we began having children, we started asking God how to raise them and prepare them for their destinies – we had no idea!

Before the girls approached dating, we desired, and knew we needed, a plan. How could we possibly assist them through their dating years and help get them to the altar as virgins without completely alienating them from us, or worse, from God? How could we help them to marry godly men who would love them and cherish them and encourage them to be all God had created them to be?

We knew that "(we) have not because (we) ask not" (James 4:2) so we started asking! We wanted to know God's plan for dating, courtship, and engagement. If our girls were going to have it better than we did, we needed to see to it that they went through this process His way because our way was too difficult and painful!

As always, our loving Father was right there to give us the truth and wisdom we needed.

Chapter 2

The Destiny Factor

Joel: I have come to the conclusion that many Christians do not believe in dating. I'm not against dating, but I am against any kind of dating without a simple, clear, godly plan, a practical, proven plan for successful dating with destiny in mind. I am against dating that is reckless, leaving broken hearts and destroyed innocence in its wake. God is smart, and He knows what we face with our kids today. He has a design for dating, and that's what this book is about.

God's plan for dating has distinct, loving boundaries. The goal is always right there in front of you, the parent, and that helps to guide everything in a pure and right direction. The Lord has shown us, as a family, that dating can be a lot of fun and a very positive growing experience when we all have that clear sense of direction and destiny. Because of the healing that has occurred in my heart as I have lived with and loved my own darling of destiny, my wife Linda, we have been able to truly enjoy helping our three daughters with their adventures in dating together.

This is our story, Linda's and mine, of how we learned to teach our daughters to date with destiny in mind. This is also our daughters' stories. All three of them have embraced the truth and love behind the call to date with destiny in mind. I am no expert, but I have discovered that the outline in this book not only has proved helpful to our daughters, but has been a good guide for the men they dated, as well as anyone of any age who desires to date with holy purity.

It's Contagious!

I wish you could sit down and interview the young men who have come through our lives while dating our daughters. Because this dating guideline is offered as a service to them in the spirit of love and not legalism, most of the young men have flourished in their personal lives regardless of whether or not they continued to date one of my young ladies.

I describe the dating outline to them in detail when they first decide and express that they want to date one of my daughters. Then, as the dating relationship progresses, I mentor and coach them in authentic, godly manhood as they go through all the steps. In most cases, whether or not they continue dating my daughter, they often adopt me as a spiritual father. Some have continued to call Linda and me and consider us good friends as they date other young women. This has been an unexpected and continued joy in our lives.

My experience with these young men has been that they frequently tell their friends about the dating outline and the things they are learning. It's so unique and causes their lives to progress with ease that, of course, their friends become curious. Some of them immediately see the value of the process and ask for the dating outline themselves, even though they are not dating one of my daughters. At this writing, my life is full of young men asking me to take them through the dating outline, which has been another incentive to write this book.

Why is this dating outline so contagious? The Bible says that we perish, we literally waste away in discouragement and pain, without a vision (Proverbs 29:18). Without a plan we are just drifting through life like I was as a teenager. We allow the enemy to break our hearts and destroy our innocence and purity because we don't know there is any other way. I am convinced that most young men and women today are feeling just like that! This is why the response to our dating outline has been so amazing. Our dating outline is "dating with destiny in mind." It brings a powerful focus and meaning to the whole dating experience.

I am not exaggerating when I say that the results of this life-giving outline speak for themselves. I can't keep up with the requests from young men and young women who want a "life-coach" or a "spiritual father" who will lovingly help walk them through what I call the seasons and levels of the dating experience.

On rare occasions I hear of people who have been unable or unwilling to understand the spirit and value of the dating outline - some have never tried it, but have scoffed at what we have committed ourselves to do by following it. Regardless, we simply pray they will seek God for the plan that will help their families, yet we know the one He gave us works! Furthermore, it has worked for countless other families. We have "field-tested" it with young men and women who are not our children, and the results have been very good and gratifying for everyone involved.

When something is as effective, and fun, as our dating outline, it's no wonder it seems to be contagious.

The Value of Purity and Innocence

The skeptics and cynics that do not see any benefit in, and even sometimes disapprove of, the dating outline are easy to understand. We live in a society that no longer values purity and innocence in adults, and sometimes even in children. Movies and television promote sex outside of marriage - they present sexual promiscuity as a normal lifestyle. Unfortunately, to wait to have sex after marriage is highly suspect in the world's eyes.

Many children today have single parents who are co-habiting with someone, or who have "sleepovers" with someone outside of the marriage covenant. Some even profess to be Christians! I believe these children instinctively know what is right and what is wrong because the Bible indicated that God's laws of purity and innocence are written in their hearts. However, it doesn't take long for the world to convince these innocent ones that what they knew to be true as children was just a smoke-screen. They lose their pure and virtuous thinking, and then they lose all purity and innocence in their lives.

The world says, "Ahhhh, isn't that sweet," when there is an innocent baby or a young child around, but if a teenager or an adult is innocent and pure, they are labeled "weird." They are seen as ignorant, too sheltered, and are told that they are "missing it." What are they missing? Simply stated, hell on earth, but the world is not going to advertise that.

One of the redeeming aspects of my personal process of recovery from impurity has been the reawakening and realization of how precious and powerful our righteousness is. I have discovered you can be very well informed, intelligent, and cool, yet still manage to maintain your child-like faith and purity of soul. This is something today's "modern thinkers" don't want anyone to know. They don't value innocence and they do nothing to protect it in our society. Furthermore, they will subtly, or sometimes aggressively, persecute and mock churches and believers who value purity and innocence.

As usual, the enemies of our souls and lives have overplayed their hands. Too many men and women have "crash and burn" stories in their past, much like mine. Too many young people are seeing the heartbreak and devastation in their parents' lives, or are experiencing it themselves. They are crying out for someone to give them truth that they can be certain of, wisdom to guide them through any situation, and love and understanding that will never fail them.

That is why our simple, little dating outline is of such interest to others. People are desperate for something and Someone they can believe in. That something is the Bible, and that Someone is Jesus! He is the way, the truth, and the life, and He is the only way to know our loving, wise Heavenly Father (John 14:6). This means He is the greatest dating and life coach anyone can have!

Instinctively and intuitively, people know the value of innocence and purity. They know that remaining virtuous produces a life of confidence, direction, and freedom. Have you ever noticed that the people who live in authentic purity of heart are truly happy and productive?

The world works overtime to claim that innocence and purity result in intellectual ignorance and a lack of necessary experience, but that is a lie. I dare you to introduce me to a person who lives in moral depravity and is both happy and productive. Yes, sin is fun for awhile, but eventually it destroys your life.

The value of innocence and purity of heart in a person's life is that they produce joy and success on every level, in every area, including dating and marriage.

A Proven Plan

The longer I live and the sweeter my walk with Jesus becomes, the more I realize how reckless and unfortunate it is that so many of God's children of destiny move through adolescence and into dating relationships without a clear vision or roadmap for dating and courtship.

Young men and women have destiny written on their hearts by God, and deep down inside they desire guidance and wisdom. They want to know the right way, the absolute truth, and a life of eternal love and security. In a practical, everyday sense, they want the tools without legalism and religious straitjackets. They want relationship and life-giving direction offered in love and dialogue. Most young people have a strong sense of destiny and they thrive when someone loving and trustworthy offers to help them reach their destiny. That's why they aren't afraid of godly help in dating.

With very few exceptions each young man my daughters have brought to my door has flourished under a planned approach to dating. Most importantly, rather than being their "adversary" as they dated my daughter, we found ourselves becoming a loving team, working together to achieve our goals and fulfill our destinies.

In the dating outline, we have described common goals for the common good. It's not difficult to build a "win-win-win" relationship with this outline. The parents win, the boyfriend wins, and the daughter wins. My advice to you is to take a look at the outline offered here and see if some of the ideas work for you - use what you like and adapt it to your life for a plan that prospers you and your precious relationships. I truly believe God will bless and help you as you enter the adventure of dating with destiny in mind.

Chapter 3

The Power of Godly Affection

Linda: In the very last book of the Old Testament, God tells us that in the Last Days, right before the Day of Judgment, He will do something so miraculous that the whole world will sit up and take notice. He is going to "turn the hearts of the fathers to their children and the hearts of the children to their fathers" (Malachi 4:6). Just to make sure we heard this, He talks more about the same thing in the New Testament, in the book of Luke.

In Luke 1:16-17 God says something really powerful and relevant to what families are going through today. He says:

"Many of the people of Israel will he bring back to the Lord their God. And he will go on before the Lord, in the spirit and power of Elijah, to turn the hearts of the fathers to their children and the disobedient to the wisdom of the righteous — to make ready a people prepared for the Lord." (NIV)

One of the things God loves to do is to bring parents and children together — no matter the age-span. If you are a Christian parent who wants to help your kids get through their dating years successfully, you must bring the Father's unconditional love and affection into your family. You have the power to do this no matter what your situation - whether you are a single parent or married, you can learn to receive the Father's love, live in it, and give it away, with affection, to your children.

The Bible indicates that one sign of authentic revival is the restoration of peace and joy in families. It's one thing to have people "stirred" by the Holy Spirit in the church building, but is His love, presence, and power manifesting in the homes. We want the Father's love to manifest even in the relationships within our families. We want it to manifest as we live and conduct business in our community. That's how we know, and how everyone else will know, that the Holy Spirit has really touched and changed our lives.

Let's take a closer look at what the Bible says are the genuine signs of people being touched by God. I have discovered four of them, and each one of them has a great impact on the whole issue of dating.

1.   Fathers' hearts turn back to their kids.

It is a beautiful thing to see a father show real love, care, and concern for his children. Unfortunately, in today's world it is also a rare thing.

I grew up in a home that was very dysfunctional. My father didn't act like he cared about me at all. He was mean and did mean things to me. I did not have a loving and affectionate relationship with him at all.

As a precious little girl I could not understand living without my dad's love, and I was way too young to understand that he was probably a wounded child himself. All I knew was that my little heart was crying out for my father to love me. Inside

I was screaming, "Could you please just hold me and love me? Could you tell me that you like me, just once? Please tell me you're glad I was born and that you think I'm pretty. I'm growing into a woman right before your eyes, and I long for you to hold me in your arms and tell me I'm special!"

I praise God that my father later came to know Jesus, but while I was growing up I would have done anything to have him put his arm around my shoulders or kiss me on the cheek. Instead, he often told me I was "no good" and even tried to sell me to his friends when my body began to develop into a woman. That is not normal family life! That is the result of a heart that is hard toward God, and only He can cleanse it, free it, and fill it with His powerful and life-changing love and affection.

We all need fathers and mothers who will love us, nurture us, and take care of us. We need both a mom and a dad, and I promise you, whether it's a little boy or a little girl, they're looking to fathers for love and affection just as much as they are looking to their mothers for love and affection.

Also, I had never received any direction from my parents. We lived on a farm in the country, and looking back I can see how that probably kept me safe. I was left to entertain myself and pretty much do as I pleased. No one cared where I was or what I did. With hindsight, I thank the Lord now that before I even knew Him, before I knew about salvation or had heard the name of Jesus, He sent His angels to watch over me as a child and as a young lady.

Then came that great day when I accepted Jesus and my life took on a purpose and a meaning for the first time! I went on my journey of discovering the depths of the Father's love and affection for me. Now I read in the Bible that in these "Last Days" the Holy Spirit is going to "turn the hearts of fathers to their children" (Malachi 4:6). So I asked the question, "What does that really look like?" The answer I found is that it is true revival.

When true revival hits a group of people, fathers change the way they have previously done things: they rearrange their work schedules in order to spend more time with their kids, they help them with their homework, talk with them and pray with them every day, and take an interest in what their kids are interested in.

Because God is talking about a dad's heart, however, the change goes much deeper than simply changing their schedules or altering their calendars to spend more time with their families. This personal revival results in a greater show of affection and love toward their children. He calls this revival because fathers are acting like THE FATHER in heaven!

In more and more families, fathers are absent or leave raising the children to the mothers, or even grandparents. There are some cultures who have always done it this way, but this is not truly God's way. Christian families must line their lives up according to the Word of God, and that may require leaving one's culture and traditions behind. Joel and I can tell you that anything you give up to love and serve God, and to love and lead and serve the children in your life, is worth it! What you get in return is a happy and healthy family, where each member is fulfilling their divine destiny.

2.   The Father's love and affection crushes
       rebellion and causes kids to turn their
       hearts to the "wisdom of the
       righteous."

When parents express authentic affection toward their kids in loving acts, like listening and trying to understand their point of view, being actively involved and taking an interest in what their kids care about, giving them counsel and direction, and correcting them when they need it, something miraculous happens. Kids will actually respect, appreciate, and are even grateful for what their parents are doing in their lives.

One of the promises that stems from God's Word is that a parent's affection toward their child becomes a gravitational pull on that child's heart to look to the parent for wisdom and guidance. Wow! The draw of authentic affection is like a compass needle being pulled to true- north. The truth is this: authentic intimacy and loving attention always trumps rebellion.

God's Word indicates that if children have a choice between consistent, demonstrated affection from a parent or rebellion with their friends, they will choose authentic love. The key is for parents to draw upon the Father's love so they can consistently express this authentic affection and love to their kids.

Have you ever considered why it is that we can come into the four walls of the church and hug each other, love each other, even talk nice to each other and listen to each other, encourage each other with life-giving words, teach each other, comfort each other, and pray for each other, but then in our own homes we're not capable of being nice to each other? The blunt honesty concerning the matter is that it's really not that hard to make the choice to show affection in our homes, toward our own families.

Making that choice means we must be determined to get healed ourselves. That's the key! We have to get rid of our own hurt, pain, anger, and bitterness in exchange for the Father's love, which can then flow through us. The Good News is that He wants to get us totally free of every issue in our past that hinders us and keeps us trapped in our pain - He will help us get delivered. Then, instead of passing on our pain and bondage, we will pass on His love, His wisdom, and His joy to our kids.

Everything starts with you. If you are having trouble with your kids, you can't expect change to come from them. You are the adult so the change has to come from you. Simply start by asking the Holy Spirit to come in power and teach you about your Father God and His affection for you right now. Begin to open up to His powerful affection and let Him change you. Don't settle for a theology about the love of God - ask the Holy Spirit to give you the reality and experience of the Father's love. If His love isn't real to you, you will never be real to your children. Only the genuine love of the Father is going to be that magnet of godly affection that will draw your kids' hearts to the wisdom and guidance you have for them.

The Bible talks about the fact that the Holy Spirit in us gives us the legal right and supernatural ability to cry, "Abba! Father!" (Galatians 4:6). The Holy Spirit is also called the "Spirit of Adoption"

(Romans 8:15), indicating to us that we are not orphans! He makes us one with our Father God and we have a heavenly Father who loves us, both now and for eternity.

If you are identifying with this in your current condition, I encourage you to renounce an "orphan spirit" and welcome "the Spirit of Adoption." Allow the Holy Spirit to do His job by confirming the reality that you are God's beloved son or daughter. Let Him fill you with God's love so you can walk in love toward your kids. Your godly affection toward them will cause them to look to you instead of rebellious peers for direction.

All of us have hurts from the past, and we recognize that hurting people will only hurt people even more. But it is the wise person who makes the choice to get healed, no matter what the cost. In the same manner, we also recognize that healed and whole people will love people and will bring God's healing. As parents, you can raise up healed and whole children who bring healing and love to others.

Dad, you are the key - you are the one who needs to humble yourself and lead the way. All eyes are on you! Everybody in the family looks to you to see what you're going to do. Start by repenting of your past sins and mistakes, asking for and receiving forgiveness, and allowing tenderness and affection to come into your heart from God so you can give it to your wife and kids. You set the tone for the home. When you do this your wife and children will begin to blossom - they will shine like stars and be the joy of your life.

If you are a single mom, the same principle applies: if you get healed and whole, your children will be healed and will become whole. If you walk in godly affection, your kids will be drawn to your wise counsel and direction. Your spiritual husband, Jesus, will help you overcome all the challenges of your situation, and you can take heart in this: the Bible promises that God will be a Father to your children … "a father to the fatherless" (Psalm 68:5).

But if you are a father, I'm asking you to go out of your way from this day forth to hug your kids, to hold them, to kiss your sons and daughters. Don't just shake their hand or slap them on the back, instead kiss them and show them deliberate affection.

I was only six years old, playing house with my dolls, and I would make up stories about having a husband who loved me and kids I would love. I was going to hold them and show them affection. I purposed then that I was going to talk nicely to them and was going to give them some direction in life. I was only six years old having these thoughts, but Jesus was preparing me to rise up and bring change to my family line.

We all need godly affection, which involves love and acceptance and forgiveness. If you know you are incapable of freely expressing affection to your spouse or kids, don't excuse yourself and don't deny the truth. Instead, embrace the truth and allow the Holy Spirit to adopt you. Don't settle for anything less than a healed up heart. Then you will be free to express authentic affection to the people you love the most.

3.   A family that has drifted from God
      will come back to Him because of the
      Father's love.

When our oldest daughter got married, many
relatives I hadn't seen for years came to the wedding.
I had prayed for these family members since I had
received Jesus at fourteen years of age. Even after all
this time, as we were doing the wedding ceremony
for our daughter and her husband, I had the
opportunity to preach and give an altar call. My
relatives came to Jesus – the best celebration of love!

In a move of God, the Father's love will reach
out through you and your family. Your immediate
family will so change that your relatives won't be
able to go without Jesus any longer. They will begin
to say, "We want what you have," because love is
contagious! They don't want dead, lifeless religion.
Authentic love and godly affection is hard to turn
down.

When family, friends, neighbors, and even co-
workers see how your wayward, rebellious children
come back into line, they are going to want the very
thing that caused this miracle in your family. In this
day and age, in our culture today, having kids that
are obedient, respectful, loving, and giving is a
miracle, but it is this very miracle that will draw all
the people in your life to God.

No matter what is transpiring with your
relatives, your neighborhood, or in your city, don't
give up hope. When you choose to serve the Lord
and love others with godly affection, you will make a
huge impact on your family and everyone you come

into contact with. It doesn't matter what kind of sin they've been involved in because the love of Jesus is more powerful than any kind of sin.

I am a living testimony of this. In one generation my family line has been turned into a godly family! My dad used to be the kind of man who wanted to deliberately hurt other people, but then my brother and I came to Jesus, followed by my mom, and then three years later my dad did also. Now the whole family is saved and there is godly affection flowing all over the place! All this happened simply because Joel and I decided to get our hearts healed and love our kids like our Father God loves us.

4.   Authentic, effective leadership operates out of a fathering and mothering heart relationship.

The fourth sign of an authentic move of God and a sign of true revival is a "fathering spirit" and "mothering spirit". Just like we need mothers and fathers in the home, we absolutely have to have mothering and fathering in the church. Joel and I are blessed to have authentic "spiritual fathers" and "spiritual mothers". The Lord has connected us with several godly men and women who are a little older and farther along in their walk with God, and who speak the truth in love to us.

We love our spiritual moms and dads. They teach us many things through relationship, and we love just being around them. We know we have someone to go to who will give us godly counsel, who will speak into our lives and pray us through whatever situation we find ourselves in.

In our own church, as the senior pastors we fill the role of spiritual mom and spiritual dad for many, but we have also raised up many leaders with a mothering and a fathering spirit. Leadership without the anointing of the Father's love is not life-changing and life-giving leadership; however, leaders who walk in the Father's love make a powerful impact on every person they touch.

The Bible tells us, and Jesus showed us, that we must take care of each other in authentic love. We can be firm and uncompromising when it comes to the Word of God, but never with a heavy hand. Too many precious believers have been wounded and hurt because leaders "laid down the law" without showing any kind of genuine affection and concern - there was no relationship. Instead of being a father or mother in the faith, they were being a dictator of dead religion. But thankfully, our Father is in the business of shattering all our religious nonsense and changing hearts through both truth and love. He is bringing forth the kind of leaders who will gently and prayerfully guide us, correct us, instruct us, encourage us, nurture us, and even lovingly admonish or rebuke us from time to time.

There is nothing like being rebuked by genuine love. When someone genuinely loves you and cares about you, and they gently tell you that you are on the wrong path or that you have sinned in some way, you are more likely to listen. That's why godly affection is a vital key to getting our kids through the dating years in victory.

It's not going to be a heavy, cold hand that brings your children into their destiny. If this is their reality, they are not going to respond the way you want them to respond. If you show no respect and love for them, later, when they begin to go through the teenage years, they will most likely move as far away from your guidance and instruction as possible. They will probably rebel against everything you stand for. But if you allow God to turn your heart to their hearts, and you begin to show them godly affection and loving respect, when you speak the truth in love they will listen. They will turn from their rebellious (and miserable) friends and gladly come back to your loving arms!

Any human being will gladly follow, listen to, and learn from a spiritual father or mother who has genuine love for them. This is why godly affection is the foundation for the dating outline the Holy Spirit gave Joel and me for our girls. It is the foundation in which the Holy Spirit will also give you a plan to guide your children through the process of dating with destiny in mind.

My Part in the Dating Outline

When Joel and I began to have children, like he stated earlier, we didn't know how exactly to raise them. So I read a lot of books on how to parent, and I would tell Joel everything I was learning so we could put our best foot forward. These books would say things like, "As your little girls start getting older, they need you to hug them and to not be afraid of them. They're not so delicate that they're going to break. They need you to demonstrate how much you love them."

Because my experience as a little girl was just about the opposite of what I am describing that needs to take place, and because I knew I had really missed something great, I went out of my way to love and be affectionate with our three daughters. I would tell Joel, "You can't overdo it on loving our girls. Just give them a whole lot of love and affection whenever you are around them."

When our oldest daughter started junior high I told Joel, "Now you have to change how you do it. You've got to start making her feel like a young lady. You have to let her know that you're Dad, and you're guiding and watching over her as she begins to notice boys and start talking with them on the phone. You have to assure her that you think she is very special and beautiful."

Joel and I began to work on developing a plan with our girls so they would feel safe in their dating years. We wanted them to feel free to venture outside of our reach and explore life, but we knew they couldn't feel secure and safe without guidance from us. We also wanted our instruction, direction, and even our correction to come across to them in love. We didn't want to have strict control or a heavy hand, rather, we wanted to operate with clear rules and consequences grounded in love.

We prayed over this plan a lot, and we feel that God gave us a great one. As a result, when our daughters got older and young men wanted to date them, it became a very exciting time because we were prepared and they were prepared. We weren't scared of what might happen to them and we weren't afraid they were going to rebel and get into all kinds of terrible trouble. Instead, we tackled the whole dating process head-on so that the enemy never had a chance to establish his influence and spoil it for any of us. It is not in a spirit of pride or legalism that we report to you that all three of our daughters made a choice that they wanted to be virgins on their wedding day. It was their choices, their desires, their goals and they reached their goals!

Gratefully, we never experienced one bit of rebellion from our girls through the dating years. We don't attribute this to being smart, we recognize it was because we were prepared. We had prayed and studied and God had given us a plan. We had faith and we honestly believed that the plan God had given us would work because it was His plan!

Our daughters have all had safe dating relationships, and they couldn't wait to come home and share their experiences with us after each date instead of hiding everything from us in fear, resentment, or shame. From early on, Joel and I discovered that we set the tone for the whole process. It was up to us to establish an atmosphere of love and trust. We studied the four points I discussed earlier and allowed the Father to fill us with His love and affection for our daughters so their hearts would seek us out for wisdom and instruction. Instead of being dictatorial, cold, and religious, we developed an affectionate relationship based on mutual understanding.

Some parents make a big mistake by thinking that if they are a friend to their child, their child will never rebel and will always trust them, but their kids don't need another friend - that is not what God has called them to be! Kids need a mother and a father to love them, to tell them the truth, to guide them, to correct them, and to help them pursue and reach their destiny. That's what Joel and I have always tried to do. We have tried to be the best godly parents our daughters could have.

Because we told each of them the truth in love and showed them the same respect God shows us, each of our girls easily embraced the plan God gave us. It was offered out of genuine love, affection, and honor for them and their God-given destinies. If you were to ask them today, each one of them will tell you how they have been greatly blessed by it as well.

In the following chapters, Joel is going to take you through the dating outline God gave us. I pray and believe it will be as much of a blessing to you as it has been to our family and the other couples and families who have used it.

Chapter 4

Step One:
Celebrate Your Child

Joel: When we saw our daughters transitioning from little girls into young women, we didn't ignore it and we didn't pretend it wasn't happening. We decided to celebrate it, to capture it, to embrace it, and to declare that it was a good thing.

The Bible says that "perfect love casts out fear" (I John 4:18), so Linda and I decided to love our girls through the teenage years instead of being intimidated by this period of growth and transition. Many parents are afraid when their children become teenagers, but God reminds us that love is stronger than rebellion. We can love our children through these years, and they can be the most wonderful years of our lives.

How did we do that? When our oldest daughter, Cristin, was twelve and about to turn thirteen, Linda and I decided I would take Cristin on a special date to celebrate her becoming a young woman. I credit Linda for helping me figure this out and plan this event because she really understood how important and necessary a father's love is to a daughter. Along the way, I discovered that if I "romanced" my daughter the way Jesus "romances" us, then I would be the number one guy in her life. If I had her heart, she would compare every other guy to me and the standard that was set by how I treated her.

For her thirteenth birthday, I gave Cristin a card which read, "Honey, I want to take you on your first date, just you and me. In this box you will find a beautiful dress. Mom will help you to get your hair all fixed up so that you feel as beautiful as you are. Tomorrow night, I'm going to pick you up for our date and take you to the nicest restaurant in town."

"Oh, yes, Daddy!" she exclaimed when she read the card and opened her birthday present to see her new dress.

For the next twenty-four hours I talked all about our date. I would say things like, "Oh, I can't wait! It's going to be so cool! We're going to have so much fun." I talked about it every moment I could. "Our date is going to be the best date you've ever been on." I did everything I knew and said everything I could say to sweep her off her feet.

On the morning of the date, I said, "This is the day! Don't be late! I'll be here." Late that afternoon I came home from work, put on my best suit, got in the car, picked up some flowers and returned home. At the appointed time, I came to the door, made sure I looked good, and knocked on the door. Cristin opened it, her precious face shining. I gave her a beautiful flower bouquet and said, "Honey, you look so beautiful! Oh, my heart, my heart! You are a beautiful woman. Are you ready for the date?"

She smiled and said, "Yes," as she rushed into my arms.

I offered her my arm, as a gentleman would, and escorted her to the car. I opened the door for her, she got in, and then I stopped before closing her door. I said, "In the future, young men are going to ask you for a date, and when you go to the car, if they don't open the door for you, just stand there and look at them with a look that says, 'What's wrong with you?'"

"Okay, Dad."

This was just a small thing, but it is an important thing. From that moment on, my daughter could tell right away if her date was a considerate man or not. If he didn't open doors for her, bring her flowers, tell her she looked beautiful, and treat her like she was a princess, she would come home and say, "I don't know what is the matter with him. He isn't my kind of guy," and I would just smile inside because I knew what she was really saying, "He's not at all like my dad!"

During the date we ate without being nervous. We held hands, and we talked about all kinds of things that were of interest to her. Finally, I would announce the celebration. I begin by asking her, "Do you know why we're here?"

Her reply: "Because you love me."

I answered, "Yes. And we also want to celebrate. Today you are a woman. And your mom and I love that you're a woman, but you'll always be my little girl and you'll always be my favorite girl."

I tell all my daughters, "You're my favorite," and I tell them all that I tell the others too because they're all my favorites. In this way, I'm trying to be like God. I love all my children and I have a big heart. If I had more children, they'd be my favorites too!

I continued, "We're here to celebrate you. We're glad that you're a woman. God loves women. He thinks they're precious. We see that you're changing. You're becoming an adult, and we bless you. We think it's good that you're becoming a young woman, and we're going to start treating you more like an adult. We're going to give you more choices, and if you do well with those choices, then you will get even more. But if you do poorly, you will get fewer choices."

This is like introducing a new game to her, and she says, "Okay. This'll be fun."

Now I have completed Step One: I have established the truth that she is becoming a woman, God loves and cherishes women, this is a very exciting and wonderful time of her life, and her mother and I are really happy and excited for her. We want her to enjoy this part of her life and to grow and to flourish in it. She is going to be given opportunities and choices, and if she handles them well, she will be given more.

I have set the stage for Step Two.

Chapter 5

Step Two:
Begin With the End in Mind

Joel: While I am still sitting with my daughter at the restaurant, I ask her this question: "Have you ever thought about what your wedding day would look like?" And she says "Yes!" of course. If you have a son, he may need some encouragement to think and talk about it, but generally the girls have thought about it and have a lot of ideas to share.

Then I say, "On your wedding day, do you want to wear white? Would you like to walk down the aisle in a beautiful white dress?"
She says, "Of course!"

I ask, "Why would a bride wear white?"

She answers, "Purity." All three of our girls have said this because Linda and I are very open and honest about this. If you have never discussed being sexually pure with your children, now would be a good time!

I continue, "That's right. That's good. So you would like to be a virgin on your wedding day?"

Each of my three daughters, when asked this question, has looked at me like, "Well, of course, duh!"

"That's great, Honey. So you are going to start this process of becoming a woman and beginning to date with the end in mind. That's very wise! Now, if you want to be a virgin on your wedding day, we need to make some decisions today."

"Okay."

"You have already made a very good decision to be a virgin when you are married, but I have to tell you the truth. I don't think you can make it without our help. Mom and I have gone through this, you know, and it can be very difficult to remain pure in the world we live in, especially as you become more interested in boys and your body begins to develop. The devil, the boy you like, and your own flesh are going to try to get you to do just the opposite of what you want to do. Do you understand what I'm talking about?"

"Yes, Dad."

"Mom and I have talked about this, and we don't think you can remain pure on your own. So if that's your goal, would you let us help you reach that goal?"

On behalf of her mother and me, I am asking my daughter's permission for us to be the respected authority in her life until she reaches her goal of marrying as a virgin. This is not trickery, and it's not manipulation. I have simply done what God does with us - He tells us the truth and expresses His desire to help us fulfill our destiny.

In the same way, I have laid out the facts to my daughter: she is young, she has made a great choice to be married a virgin, but her spiritual enemies, the world we live in, and her flesh will do everything they can to keep her from meeting that goal; therefore, her mother and I have a desire to help her reach her goal, just like God wants to help us reach our goals.

What do you think each one of our daughters has said? "Well, of course I want your help!"

With their permission, Linda and I are now in the door. She has made us her dating and relationship "coaches". She wants our help to reach her goal to remain pure for her husband.

Every one of our daughters has seen the truth and wisdom in this. Each has gladly and gratefully accepted our offer to help them. And so Linda and I have received our daughters' permission to be their coaches in dating and relationships.

It is now time for Step Three.

Chapter 6

Step Three:
Make a Covenant of Love
and Purity

Joel: On the big date with my daughter, so far I have celebrated her coming into womanhood, I've told her the truth about this time of her life, that it is a wonderful time but also a very challenging time, and I have obtained her permission for her mother and me to help her go through it and reach her goal to be married a virgin. Now I will move on to Step Three.

At this point, I took out a little gift box that I had kept hidden in my pocket and I placed it in front of my daughter. I say, "Mom and I have a gift for you."

She opened it excitedly and saw a beautiful little diamond ring inside. I say, "It's called a purity ring. Have you noticed that Mom and I both wear rings?" (I show her my ring.) "Mom has a wedding ring, and I have a wedding ring. We each took a vow to love and remain faithful to each other. I'm not going to look at other women and I'm not going to have sex with other women. I'm not going to look at pornography and I don't want to have an affair. There's one woman in my life - she has captured my heart, and I'm going to keep my heart pure for her for the rest of my life.

"Your Mom wears her ring because it symbolizes that she will not look at, fall in love with, or have sex with other men. She has given her life to Jesus and to me. We - you, your sisters, and I - have her heart, and she only has to look at the ring on her hand to be reminded that she belongs only to us. She guards and protects her heart to be faithful to us, and that is what keeps her happy and makes her life wonderful.

"Your mom and I have a covenant of marriage with each other. You know that any covenant is very sacred to Jesus. Our covenant is an agreement we made to be faithful and loyal to one another, to help one another at all times and in all situations, no matter what the cost. And Jesus is right there to support us and help us keep our word to each other.

"You have seen how mom and I are not perfect, but at the same time, we live our lives in this covenant of love and purity, faithful to Jesus and to each other. We have given each other rings as a symbol of the covenant we have, and now we want to give you a ring because we want you to experience the same joy and peace. Mom and I would like to come into a covenant with you, a covenant of love and purity. A diamond is a pure stone and that's how you, as well as your mother and I, desire for you to be on your wedding day. Please know this: even if you mess up, your mother and I, and especially God, will forgive you faster that you can forgive yourself, but because we don't want you to struggle with that pain, we want you to wear this ring to remember how much we love you, how much God loves you, and how great the love will be on your wedding day when you are able to tell your husband, "I stayed pure for you," and you exchange this small diamond ring for one that is much more beautiful! Would that be okay?"

"Yes Dad!"

I put the ring on her finger and say, "This ring is yours, and it is to remind you that we love you, and we are in covenant with you. The Bible says a three-fold cord is very difficult to break. Our three-fold card is Mom—Dad—You. A covenant of three will be very difficult for the devil, or anyone else, or even your own flesh to break. Wear this ring as a symbol of our covenant of love and purity, and we will all ask Jesus to help us. I believe He will give us the wisdom and courage to succeed."

Then I say, "You're a beautiful young lady. Pretty soon young men are going to start to notice you, and they're going to want your love. That's okay, but don't give it to them — not yet! Promise me this because you want to reach your goal of purity, of being a virgin for your husband.

"When some young man is attracted to you and you find yourself attracted to him, and he wants to take you out on a date, promise me you will tell him, 'Not until you talk to my dad.'

"Yes Dad."

With a big smile I say, "You know how Jesus said 'I am the way, the truth and the life, and no one comes to the Father but by me?' (John 14:6) Well Honey, I am the way, the truth, and the life in this family, and no young man comes to my daughter but through me."

She laughs, looks at the ring on her finger and says, "Yes Dad. I promise."

I also warn her about the power of the ring she's wearing. I tell her that when a boy is interested in her, he will probably notice the ring and ask, "Are you going with anybody?"

She should answer, "Oh, that's my purity ring," and tell them about the covenant of love and purity she has made with Jesus and her parents. I warn her that many boys will stay away from her after that, but quickly tell her, "Don't worry about that. If a man really loves you, that ring will not chase him away. It will make you even more wonderful to him. And don't worry about asking him to talk to me. If he really loves you, he'll talk to me. If he won't talk to me, he is a coward, and you don't want a coward for a boyfriend!

"You also don't want a boyfriend who just wants sex from you. You want someone who loves you and knows how terrific you are! So if you tell them about our covenant and they run away from you, thank God for His protection. He's saving you from a loser and keeping you pure for the amazing guy who is to be your husband."

The date with my daughter now comes to an end. We have celebrated her step into womanhood. We have established her goal to marry as a virgin. She has given her mother and me permission to guide her through her dating years. I have given her a beautiful ring to symbolize the covenant of love and purity we have made with each other and with Jesus. And she has promised to bring any young man who wants to date her to me first. She has made me the door through which any young man must step before he can pursue her affection.

These first three steps are accomplished in one wonderful evening, but they are also the foundation for our relationship with our daughter throughout her dating years.

Chapter 7

Rite of Passage –
No Regrets

Joel and Linda: Before we go on with the dating outline, we want to suggest a life-changing event that you can do for your junior high students that will have a huge impact on them and help set the course of their heart toward a divine destiny. We call it "Rite of Passage – No Regrets".

We have observed that junior high tends to be the stage transition. This is the season when our kids begin to transform and are changing from a child into a teenager, and then a young adult. What is true in the physical can also be true in the spiritual if we wisely capture the opportunity.

In junior high, we have the opportunity to help our kids see a preferable future before they get caught up in the great deceptions of our post-Christian culture.

This is the age when Joel took our daughters on their first date because we wanted to begin to prepare them for all that is ahead in the dating scene – the good and the bad. This is also the strategic time in life when every boy and girl begins to change and go through what we call a "Rite of Passage". The goal is, let's do it without regrets.

Let us pose a question: what if you were made aware ahead of time that Satan and his demons were about to target your child with a well-camouflaged test designed to destroy their innocence and destiny? Furthermore, what if you knew exactly when that test was coming? What if you knew what the test consisted of - the questions and the temptations the forces of evil would use? Most importantly, what if you knew God had given you the answers to that test and the time to prepare your child for it? Would you prepare your child? Sure you would! What a gift and a wonderful strategic advantage from God!

That is what happens in the season of your child's life we call "Rite of Passage — No Regrets." We recommend that you take advantage of a well-designed program where your kids are told about the devil's upcoming tests, are clued-in on and prepared for the questions he will raise, and are given the answers from God's Word before the test is even given.

At our insistence, our oldest daughter, Cristin, wrote and then field-tested this "Rite of Passage" program over a period of several years. She had graduated from college with a degree in education, and we recognized she had a gift for writing curriculum. We hired her on the spot and gave her the priority of focusing her ministry efforts on junior high kids and their needs.

We specifically target the junior high span because during our twenty-five years of pastoring, we have come to recognize this as the battlefield where many parents, as well as the church, were losing the next generation without really knowing it was happening. We saw a number of common points in which many good Christian kids were being "taken out" at this strategic time of their lives, and we knew God had the answers and the strategy to stop it. Consequently, we asked our daughter to develop a rich, interesting, fun curriculum that would help safeguard kids from the deceptions, schemes, and traps the enemy was laying for them. What resulted was the "Rite of Passage — No Regrets" program.

There are now many proud graduates of the program, and both the students and their parents highly endorse it. We believe, and we can see, that this program has kept many young teenagers on track with God in a world that does everything in its power to get them away from Him, away from a life-giving church, and away from their God-given destinies.

In this program students (and parents are encouraged to actively participate and are given tools on how to do so) learn to discern the upcoming battle and battlefields for what they really are. They learn to recognize and address the temptations and pressures of this young adult world and culture. At the same time the student (and parents) are taught to locate and embrace the wonderful calling, anointing, and plan God has for their life. We help them articulate their purpose, and when they see what a great future He has for them, it becomes easier for them to choose life with God over the temptations of the enemy. The program also teaches them the value of virginity as we expose how and why "the father of lies" works so hard to de-value purity of heart and purity of the body.

Certainly you are aware that the spirit of this age is on a crusade to de-value virginity, but who, besides you, is going to raise up the exciting adventure of more purity with a purpose? They need to hear it from more voices and commit to purity because they see the value of it. While the world makes fun, ridicules, mocks and tries to embarrass the young men and women for being virgins, we raise the voice of Truth and expose the lie of, as well as the consequences of, sexual impurity. This program says what needs to be said about virginity: it's a gift, it's a freedom, and it's safety; it's beauty, it's innocence, and it is wonderful! At the very least, it's God's call and standard.

The student (and parents) also participate in breaking generational iniquity patterns and ungodly soul-ties with the seductive options this world offers. The student is guided in preparing a personal mission and purpose statement, including choosing a "life verse" from God's Word as the target and focus of their future. Their mission statement investigates and lays claim to their spiritual heritage as a Christ follower. We also help the student to set meaningful, godly goals for their life — and much more!

The culmination of this experience is a deeply moving, formal, anointed "Rite of Passage" ceremony to be witnessed and shared with friends and family members. This is a special time when parents lay hands on their child and transfer "the blessing." Then we have a planned reception immediately following, with a few planned activities, to celebrate not only graduation from the class, but also their entrance into the adventure of being an authentic godly man or woman.

This is more than just a wonderful program - this is a season in your child's life where the tone can be set to become young adults who live with destiny in mind. They will know in advance how to approach and deal with the opposite sex and all the temptations of this world in a godly way. And, as we said before, after this program they will have such a beautiful picture of who they are in Christ and what He has for them, that they will gladly choose His way to walk in their destiny.

If a mom and dad would do what you just read in steps one, two and three in this book with their son and daughter and then do "Rite of Passage – No Regrets" with that child in the same season of development, there would be such closeness and clarity for both the child and the parents that the foundation would be solid for future healthy growth.

In case you think junior high "kids" can't set significant goals at this age, you are mistaken. This is the age when our youngest daughter saw her older sisters dating and on her own set the goal before God and prayed: "I don't want to date anyone who isn't going to be my husband. Jesus, would you please work that out in my life?"

We thought that goal was a little too unrealistic and childish. Evidently, God loved it. Haley's first date and only boyfriend from high school to the altar was the man who became her husband, Chris, and they both were virgins on their wedding day and they are both living their dreams today.

If you would like to receive the curriculum for "Rite of Passage — No Regrets," we have provided information at the back of this book in the "Toolbox" section.

Perhaps you think we are a little "overboard" with all this emphasis on capturing the heart of the junior high young person, or perhaps you think they are too young to care about purity and destiny and dating. Just ask a junior high school teacher or a junior high youth pastor to read these seven or eight chapters and tell them to speak their minds. They will open your eyes to the need and the desperate cry for a "Rite of Passage" – "No Regrets."

Chapter 8

Step Four:
The Talk

Joel: My girls call Step Four "The Talk." In Step Three each daughter has promised to bring any young man who desires to begin dating to me first. I want to have a talk with him and get to know him a little because I am not going to let my daughter date just anyone. She is far too valuable and precious to me!

Allow me to reply the scene for you: One day a young man comes to the door, introduces himself, and says, "Could I talk to you?"

I say, "Sure. What about?" I pretend that I don't know why they're there.

"Well, uh ... uh ... I want to go out with your daughter."

"So you want to date my daughter? Well, I can see why. She's a beautiful girl. Come on in and we'll talk about it."

I take him to the kitchen table and call out to Linda, "Mom, someone's here. He wants to date your daughter." Then I call to the daughter in question, saying, "Come here, please. There's a guy here who wants to date you." All four of us sit at the table together.

First, I begin with small talk. "How are you? How old are you? What's your favorite sport? Tell me about yourself." I try to get the young man to open up and relax a little so he will talk.

Next, I ask this question: "If you could have any car in the world, what would it be? What's your dream car?" He always knows exactly what he wants. Sometimes I might ask, "Why do you like that car?" But generally every young man wants a car, and he can tell me every detail about his car without me pressing him.

Then I will ask, "Would you like a brand new one?" His eyes shine when he says yes. And then I say, "Pretend you get that car. Then one day I come over to your house and I ask if I can borrow your car. What would you say?"

Some laugh and say no. They think I'm joking around with them. Others try to impress me and say, "Oh sure, you can borrow my car anytime."

It doesn't matter what the guy says. I just go on, saying, "Let's pretend you let me borrow your dream car, your favorite car in the world. I drive it away in the late afternoon, and when I bring it back that night, what condition do you want your car to be in?"

He may catch what I'm really saying right away, then again, He might not be so quick, but I always say this, "When I bring your car back, do you want it full of garbage and covered with filth? Do you want it dirty inside and outside?"

"Oh no, I want it clean."

Then I make the point clear. "Your car is to you almost as important as my daughter is to me. When you bring my daughter home after a date, I want her clean. Right now she's clean - she's spiritually clean, she's mentally clean, and she's emotionally clean. She's physically pure, a virgin.

When she comes back from dating you, I want her clean. Understand? No fingerprints."

"Yesssir."

"Now, when I bring your car back, what about the gas tank?"

He asks, "What do you mean?"

"Well, do you want the tank to be full or do you want it to be empty?"

"I would like it full," he always says.

I say, "Good. Speaking about my daughter ... she has a spiritual tank, and right now it's full. She's hot for God and she loves God. Don't empty her tank. Bring her back full of the Spirit and on fire for God. She has an emotional tank. Bring her home full of happiness. Fill it up! And she has a mental tank. Right now she is full of God's Word, so don't bring her back all confused and full of doubts. I want you to bring her back with a full tank, just like she was when you picked her up. Understand?"

"Yessir."

I continue. "Now this car that you have, when I bring it back, how would you feel if I had a scratch or a dent on it?"

He says, "I wouldn't be happy."

"Okay, we're talking about my daughter now. No dents, no scratches. No damage. No wrecks. Make sense?"

By now he more than gets it. He smiles and says, "Yes, Sir." He thinks The Talk is over, but then I launch into the third phase.

"Oh, one more thing. I want to talk about boundaries. Nobody wants to talk about boundaries, but we all need to have them. And I have boundaries." I look the young man right in the eye and say, "It's real simple. Anything you would be afraid to do with me, you don't do with her. Is that clear?"

He says, "Oh, sure."

But I don't let him get off that easy. "Would you be uncomfortable kissing me on the lips?" And I start to move in close to his face, as if I were going to kiss him.

He jerks back and says, "Yes! I don't want to kiss you!"

Then I say, "Well then, don't kiss my daughter. Those lips belong to her husband. Are you married to her?"

"No!"

I say it again, "Well then, don't kiss those lips. They don't belong to you. They belong to her future husband. Many people think kissing is okay, but it stirs up physical passion. Then the passion gets stronger and stronger, and you cannot satisfy that passion without sinning against each other and against God. So why start it? Those lips are not yours. If I catch you kissing her lips, you'll be more than kissing me for a long, long time."

He is pretty subdued by this time, but there is more.

"Okay, let's talk about holding hands." I take the boy's hand and hold it in a very platonic way. "You can hold her hand." But then I begin rubbing his hand seductively and he immediately tries to pull his hand away. I hold on and say, "Does this make you uncomfortable?"

"Yes!!!" I let go and say, "Well then, don't do it with my daughter!"

At this point he is either ready to run or is laughing nervously. Things are about to get much worse for him, however. I take his hand and place it on my knee. Then I begin to move his hand slowly up my thigh. "Does this make you uncomfortable?"

They always jerk their hands away at this point and yell, "Yes!"

"Then don't do it with my daughter! Ever!"

I stand up and motion for him to stand up. He thinks this awful "talk" is finally over. I say, "Let's talk about hugging."

His eyes open wide, terror is on his face, and he says, "Oh, no." But I grab him in a bear hug and then start slowly rubbing his back, moving downward. "Does this make you uncomfortable?"

All he says is "Ahhhh!!!"

I let go and say once more, "Then don't do that with my daughter! You can hug her like this," and I give him a nice godly hug with a pat on the back, letting go after just a few seconds. "But if you touch body parts when you hug, you and I will be touching body parts!"

While we are standing I say, "You can kiss her on the cheek," and I give him a quick, godly kiss on the cheek with a manly pat on the back. "That's not so bad, is it? It's okay, you can do that." Then I say, "Do you think you should kiss her on the neck?" and I move in like I'm going to kiss him on the neck.

"No!" And he slides away from me.

"That's called boundaries. Anything you would be uncomfortable doing with me, you'd better be uncomfortable doing that with my daughter. Why? Because it's not God's way, which means it's not clean, it's not healthy, it's not natural, and it's not normal. The world will tell you that it's natural and normal, but it's not. And all you have to do is look at the lives of people who do those things to see that they are confused and their lives are full of unclean drama and unhappiness.

"What I have just done should make you uncomfortable! It's sin. It's sin with you and me, and it's sin with you and my daughter. So leave it alone. Then you can enjoy your date, have lots of fun, and actually get to know one another better. Does that make sense?"

"Yessir."

Lastly I say, "One more thing before you go. Do you know what a covenant is?" If he isn't sure I explain, "A covenant is a sacred and binding agreement. The Bible says that when you make a covenant with someone and keep the covenant, you will be greatly blessed. On the other hand, if you break the covenant, you release curses on yourself."

I tell the young man about the covenant that Linda and I and my daughter have made. Then I ask him, "Would you like to be blessed?" He says yes. "Well then, help us keep the covenant. We're in a covenant of purity and love, and if you help keep the covenant, you will be blessed. Get ready for the favor of God on your life. Get ready for better grades in school. Get ready for a raise and a promotion at work. And get ready for God to come closer and bring you to higher spiritual levels of understanding.

"You are being tested while you date my daughter, and if you help keep the covenant God will see that and He will say, 'There's a covenant man!' All kinds of blessings will begin to be released into your life."

I'm serious when I tell them this! I've done this with many boys and young men. Every single one of them who has ever dated one of my daughters has been blessed and promoted. They all come back and say, "Wow, this covenant stuff really works!"

We're friends now, so I put my arm around his shoulder and say, "Remember what happens to a person who breaks the covenant. Curses are released. I'm not trying to scare you, but if you begin breaking the covenant, all kinds of bad things are going to start happening. You don't want to go there, believe me!"

"Ooookay." He will agree to anything right now, but he also knows that my daughter is something special and he'd better treat her right! He's not only dealing with a protective dad, he's dealing with God.

Linda, and each one of my daughters, has really enjoyed being there to observe how the young man handles "The Talk." We see him sweat bullets or try to act too cool, and we know that if he can get through "The Talk," he is probably okay. It tells us all a lot about the kind of person he is.

As I have said before, "The Talk" has given me many spiritual sons. All three of my daughters are happily married to men who survived and thrived because of "The Talk." And there are other young men they dated for awhile who still call me for advice and think of me as their life coach.

It seems God never gives a single blessing, He always multiplies the blessing. Not only does "The Talk" help insure that my daughter will be treated well on a date, and not only does it reveal something about a young man's character, but it has also allowed Linda and I to gain lasting relationships with many interesting and unique young men who desire a loving spiritual father in their lives.

Chapter 9

Step Five:
Casual Dating —
The Spirit of Friendship

Joel: Step Five begins during "The Talk". Before the first date, I get my daughter and the young man to promise me that if they begin to have strong feelings for each other, to sense they are genuinely in love, they will talk to me immediately. However, for now the focus of their dating relationship is to be friendship, getting to know one another.

Casual dating is a time of training, as well as a time for having fun. Your kids are having a great time, but you are coaching them and keeping close watch on certain things. They are going to learn a lot and grow a lot during the dating years, and you want to make sure they learn and grow in the right way. As their coach, you talk and pray for them every day and when needed, impart adjustments, corrections, or God's Word into the situations they face.

The first thing you are watching for and listening to is their attitude. You reward good attitudes and you discipline poor attitudes. You might say, "I've noticed your attitude is really, really good. You're doing great with this dating-thing. This is good." But if their attitude starts getting poor, you might say, "You know, I've noticed ever since you started dating, your attitude isn't very good. Do you want to keep dating? Okay then, here's a warning: better change the attitude or we're going to start cutting back on the dating, because something is hurting you."

When you notice the attitude is just not right, you open up conversation and you don't wait to do it. You find out what's going on and you remind them that you are their coach and you've gone through this yourself. You know they are unique and special, you know they are dating in a different time than you did, but human nature is still the same. The idea is to keep communication open – where you can stay transparent with them, and they will stay transparent with you in return.

When you know something is not right and they are not opening up to you for some reason, pray in the Holy Ghost daily. He knows everything that's going on in your daughter's life and the life of the boy she is dating. Plus, it usually only takes one time of saying, "Honey, the Holy Spirit told me today …," and they will know that not only are you involved in their dating life, but so is God!

Also, watch for obedience. You should be the one to set the time when they are supposed to be home and if they are one minute late, you say, "Next time you go on a date, we're going to take an hour off your time."

"What?"

"Would you like two hours taken off? I'm sorry you're late, but this is about trust and covenant, and I'm your coach. You've got to learn to respect time, to keep your promises, and to be where you're supposed to be on time. So for every minute you're late coming home from a date, you lose an hour." If you have a reputation for following through with rules and consequences, they will never be late again! Remember, be loving (don't be mean) but be strong.

You are teaching your daughter good habits of thinking and behavior. You are giving her boundaries of safety and security, but most of all, you are taking an active role as her loving coach. You are keeping your promise to help her keep the covenant of love and purity you made when you took her on her first date.

At the same time, you are also building relationship with the boy, or young man, she is dating. You don't want him to be afraid of you anymore like he was in "The Talk." You want to coach him and to help him grow and mature in the Lord, so you invite him into your family-circle. He doesn't just pick up your daughter every Friday night and that's all you see of him. No, you answer the door when he comes to pick up your daughter, you engage him in conversation, you pray with him when you know he has a need, perhaps a sickness or a challenge, and you have him to dinner or take him on a family outing. That's how many of these young men became spiritual sons to Linda and me. Every time one of these young men came to the door to pick up my daughter I hugged him. For some of these young men it was the only hug they ever got.

I have thought about this and believe these young men are starving to hear the truth from parents who live the truth. Some of them haven't even thought about what is moral or immoral, what is sinful or right — especially in the eyes of God. They may know the Lord, but many of them have never been encouraged or trained to let Him be a part of every area of their lives. Also, there are some who have heard it from their own parents, but until they hear it from someone else who they respect, they really won't take it seriously.

What we teach our daughter and her date is that God loves them and is interested in every part of their lives. Yes, sin is pleasant for a season, but it always brings misery and devastation to their lives and the lives of those they touch. That is why the Word of God tells them to stay pure in their hearts, in their minds, and in their behavior. We give them the truth that the world doesn't want them to know.

We tell them how God's plan is the only plan for true happiness and success. When a young man sees us demonstrate God's plan and hears us explain God's plan in "The Talk," when he sees us follow through on our promise to help him and my daughter keep the covenant of love and purity, he loves it. He knows by our caring attitude, and by the hugs and genuine expressions of kindness, that what we are saying and doing is not only to protect my daughter, but also to protect him. He knows that we are speaking the truth because we also love him and want God's best for him.

Linda has become a spiritual mother to many of these young men. Many still call and e-mail both of us. We teach them that even if they ever stop dating our daughter, it's no big deal because we have taught them to be a friend in a dating relationship. Casual dating isn't about sexual conquest, stroking your ego, or using someone to be more popular in school. It's about learning to be a good friend.

While our daughter and the young man develop their friendship, the initial attraction that made them want to date each other either becomes weaker or stronger as they get to know each other. They discover whether or not they are good together, if they enjoy each other's company in all kinds of situations, if their families are compatible, and if they see a future together.

If the friendship reveals they don't see a future together, or the initial attraction goes away, then we teach them the proper way to stop dating. Just stop! You can still be friends. You don't have to get upset with each other and never speak to each other again. That's how the world says it has to be done, but Linda and I tell them that as God's children, they don't have to have all that drama.

We let them know that either one can get out of the dating relationship at any time – they simply have to do it in a spirit of friendship. If one or the other is hurt in any way, it is because they have allowed their emotions to have too much power over them. This can happen, but as we coach our daughter and the young man through this process, they can end the dating relationship knowing that we still love and value them both.

Some kids go through terrible break-ups and have no spiritual and emotional support, or guidance, from their parents. Their parents are too busy, too intimidated by the whole dating scene, or just buy in to the world's lie that getting your heart broken again and again is part of growing up. Linda and I make it clear, beginning with "The Talk," that we don't follow the world's way of thinking and we believe it can be very different.

First, we are going to be involved, and second, we want to help both our daughter and the young man avoid heartbreak and destruction in their lives. We are there for them, and we will do everything we can to help them have the best dating experience they can have. With each of our daughters, and with nearly every young man who has dated them, they have all loved this way of doing things.

When kids really embrace the spirit of friendship during the dating years, they have so much fun! And we as parents don't have to be total wrecks every time they go out on a date! Also, when Step Six comes along, and they decide they want to get serious about each other, you have already helped them to establish a great foundation of friendship to build upon.

Chapter 10

Step Six:
Committed Dating —
The Spirit of Love

Joel: "Dad, I think I'm in love."

When love goes beyond friendship, that's when my daughter and the young man are to come to me. We have a talk about what it means to go from a casual dating situation to a committed dating relationship. I have already told my daughter and the young man, "When you start talking about love and say 'I love you' to each other, that's not casual dating anymore. So when you start feeling that way, come and talk to me."

I sit down with the two of them and say, "Okay, are you ready to move into committed dating?"

They might say, "What's that?" Or they might say, "Sure." Whatever their answer, I tell them exactly what committed dating is so there is no misunderstanding.

"Committed dating is when you don't want to date anybody else. It's when you renew your commitment to keep all the boundaries. Because love is growing stronger, your boundaries need to be stronger. Understand?"

"Yeah."

"Do we need to go through the boundaries again?"

The young man usually reacts immediately with, "No! No. I know the boundaries," because "The Talk" is still fresh in his mind!

"Are you keeping the boundaries? Are you having any trouble with the boundaries? I'll go over them again if you need me to."

The important thing to review in Step Six, committed dating, is that they are not only committed to each other in an exclusive dating relationship, but they are committed first to Jesus Christ. They are to stay within His boundaries of love and purity.

I remind them that many young people feel that just because now they love each other and see a possible future with each other, boundaries should go away. The world also tells them this. It talks about waiting to have sex, not until marriage, but waiting until "the right person" comes along. People think that waiting to have sex with "the right person" will make it okay. But it is not okay!

I tell my daughters, "If he hasn't proven himself trustworthy and truly loving, stood before God, your church, and your families, put a ring on your finger, and vowed to love you and cherish you for the rest of your lives — all his talk about commitment is unproven. Real commitment is proven in many ways during the dating and courtship process, but ultimately it is proven by marrying you. You will never be secure and happy with a man who doesn't give you that kind of commitment."

"Your sexual relationship can only flourish in the security of God's approval and your trust in one another, which only happens when you are married and exclusively committed to one another for the rest of your lives."

Committed dating has a purpose — to reveal just how committed two people are to one another. My daughter doesn't date anyone but this one young man - she needs to see how committed he really is to her and how committed she really is to him. He does not date anyone but her – he needs to see how committed she is to him and how committed he really is to her. This takes time and being with one another in different situations that will reveal what is really going on between them.

I have found that the temptation for most is to rush this process, but as their coach you emphasize the fact that they have to hear from God and have His will confirmed many times before they make the second most important decision in their lives. The first most important decision is surrendering their lives to Jesus, and the second most important decision is who they will marry and spend the rest of their lives with.

I let them know that it takes time to see just how spiritually, mentally, emotionally, and socially compatible they are for each other. They can excuse problems and disagreements for awhile, but only over a long period of time will they be able to work out those little differences for the best of both of them, or realize the differences are too huge to be resolved.

The spirit of love demands that the boundaries, physical boundaries and the time boundary, must be stronger than ever because that is the only way both of them can hear from God about their future, or lack of future, together. It is the only way they can see each other as they really are. In the end, the love they have developed in friendship will show them whether or not they are to be married.

Linda and I have discovered that coaching our daughters through this step has been really exciting. Since all three of our daughters are now married, we have seen them go through the committed dating time and then go on to Step Seven. But we have also seen them go through the committed dating step and end the dating relationship numerous times. Either way, we have rejoiced because our daughters found God's will for their lives.

Again, I want to emphasize the fact that "breaking-up" does not have to involve "heartbreak." Sometimes emotions are pretty strong and the heart can go through some pain, and that happened once to one of our daughters. However, with Linda and my support in place, she did not experience a deep and lasting hurt because she knew God had something better and thanked Him for protecting her from marrying the wrong person.

Sometimes Step Six reveals what is NOT God's will for your daughter's and the young man's lives, but that is a great thing! And we know that God works everything to their good, so the lessons learned in the relationship will be valuable to each of them in their futures.

At other times, Step Six reveals that the person your daughter is in a committed dating relationship with may be her future husband. I believe God will show this to the parents as well as to the kids. With each of our daughters, Linda and I have known when they were to go on with Step

Seven and we gave them our blessing and help to do so.

There is one other important thing I tell my daughter and the young man before they proceed with Step Six. "Now before you enter into the next phase of your relationship, committed dating, I want you to know something important: if you go through Step Six and find that you are totally committed to one another, that you see a future with one another, and that you are more in love than ever, you must remember that: committed dating does not lead to being engaged! You must promise me that if you want to seriously look at getting married, you will come to me first and together we will proceed with Step Seven."

At that point they are so excited about their relationship, they will agree to anything, but Step Seven can be one of the most difficult and challenging, yet rewarding steps of all. When I tell them what it is all about, some of the young men try to skip over it.

Chapter 11

Step Seven:
Prepare —
Become Marriage Material

Joel: Let me tell you about the "Jumpers." I call them "Jumpers" because they go into Step Six, become committed to my daughter, fall deeper in love, and then they want to "jump" right over Step Seven to get engaged. They have this romantic idea of showing up at the door for a regular date, surprising her with a ring, and sweeping her off her feet. I tell them, "You've seen too many romantic movies. Remember, romance does not mean irresponsible."

Two times I have had to deal with "Jumpers" this has happened. The first time the Holy Spirit alerted me as I opened the door on the young man, who had come to pick up my daughter. I greeted him with, "I feel like the Lord just told me you have a ring and you're going to ask my daughter to marry you. Is that right?" You have never seen a more surprised look on a man's face! I reminded him, "If you want to marry my daughter, you can't skip Step Seven. So keep your ring in your pocket and let's talk."

Then I reminded him what was involved in Step Seven. He said, "Oh, sure. No problem." And I never saw him again. It later turned out that we discovered he was not the man he had been pretending to be. The reason he was a "Jumper" was he wanted my daughter, but he didn't want to be exposed in Step Seven.

If a young man tries to "jump," I remind him that in Step Six I made him promise that he would not offer my daughter a ring and they would not get engaged until they came to talk to me. I also remind him the reason they are to come to me is to go through Step Seven together, which will show them whether or not they, as a couple, are marriage material for each other.

The young man says, "I want to give a ring to your daughter. I want to be engaged to her. I know we're ready!"

I say, "That's great!" And I call my daughter. "Do both of you feel this way?" They nod yes. "Fantastic! I'm for you and Mom is for you." Then I call Linda. We sit down together. "This is awesome. We are really excited for you. Now remember the next step, Step Seven?"

Sometimes they say, "No. What is Step Seven about?"

"It's called Prepare. This is where you get yourself ready for marriage. Before you get engaged, before you send out the wedding invitations and buy a dress, you prepare, you get yourself ready. Do you send a soldier into war before they go through boot camp?"

"No."

"Of course not! That's why I won't send you into an engagement, much less a marriage, without being prepared. There's nothing worse than having to take the ring back to the jewelers or having to return wedding gifts. You don't want to have to go through something like that, do you?"

"No!" they cry in horror.

"Okay, there are specific things Mom and I require you both to do before you become engaged and begin planning your wedding." Then we give them the list.

1. Know Yourselves Thoroughly.

If they haven't already, they must go through the "Breaking Free," "Restoring the Foundations" (called "Healing Week"), and "Healing of the Heart" classes at our church. These are really excellent inner healing and deliverance courses. All three of our sons-in-law finished these classes and said, "Everyone should take these!" Our daughters felt the same. By the end of these courses, they know their own, and each other's, weaknesses and strengths, and they come out more themselves, more healed up in their hearts, and more like the person God created them to be. (By the way, all of the men I have walked through this outline started taking these classes in Step Six because they wanted to grow as men, not because of a desire for engagement).

2. Finances.

They must meet with a business man in our church and give him copies of their bills, paycheck stubs, show him their checkbooks, and let him know any and all debts they have. As a couple, they must reveal every aspect of their financial situations to him. If they have a budget, they show it to him, but if they don't have one, he will help them set one. They need to know the financial condition of each other, how they are going to deal with financial matters, whether or not there is any debt, and how to keep things right and balanced regarding money issues. The businessman will also show them how to set a budget as a couple. Then, when they are married, hopefully there will be no surprises and they will be able to be good stewards of what God gives them.

After they have worked with the businessman, they are to come back to me and show me their budget. Then I ask them, "Do you know what a credit check is?" If they don't know I tell them. I explain that the credit reports will show what outstanding debts they have or have had, if they have paid their bills on time, and what their credit scores are. I say, "How someone handles their money is important. Jesus was really strong on this. We don't worship or love money, but we are to be good stewards of it. We are to use it in the right way." (This issue is what caused our first "Jumper" to disappear. To this day, my daughter thanks me for this! He was a charming young man, but he had a poor work ethic and integrity issues that he wasn't willing to face.)

I continue, "Money problems are a main cause of stress and divorce, and Jesus had a lot to say about it. This is nothing to take lightly! That's why we are dealing with your attitudes about money and how you handle your money right now. Mom and I don't want you to be divided or upset with each other in your marriage because you didn't know how to deal with money as individuals or as a couple before you got married."

3. Communication.

They are required to take a communication class together called "Effective Communication." As I said in the first chapter, Linda and I got married with no idea how to talk to one another without hurting and offending each other. Our marriage got so much better once we learned how to discuss issues, solve problems, handle disagreements, and especially develop the skill of listening to one another. I tell them, "Good communication is one of the main ingredients to a great marriage. You not only need to know how to talk to one another, but also how to listen prayerfully to one another. Communication affects all areas of your marriage."

4. Physical Health.

They are to each go and visit their doctor, get a complete physical exam, and tell each other and us the results. I say, "You need to know if either of you has a disease or a physical weakness that needs to be talked about and healed. You need to know if your fiancé has diabetes or a heart condition or HIV. You need to know if there is any history of mental illness or psychological problems. Just because one or both of you has a physical problem doesn't mean you can't get married but you need to know what you are facing and decide how you will deal with it together."

Over the years, before we developed this dating outline, Linda and I had done hundreds of weddings. Too many times, two weeks before the wedding, we would get a phone call from a bride or a groom who would say, "I'm getting married in two weeks and my fiancé just told me he/she has a sexually-transmitted disease. All the invitations are out, all the plans are made, and I've just discovered that on my honeymoon I'm going to get a sexually transmitted disease!" Please understand, these were good, Spirit-filled, sharp, intelligent, church-going believers —but they didn't go through Step Seven before they got engaged. They had sinned in their past and never dealt with it while dating.

This is one of the best parts of Step Seven: it prevents calling off the wedding at the last minute or worse, realizing you have made a terrible mistake just before or after the wedding.

5. Moral Integrity.

I will do a background check on the young man. I check his criminal record. Hopefully, if there is anything that needs to be revealed, he will have told my daughter, as well as Linda and me, by now. This may or may not be a factor in their eventually becoming engaged. After all, how many of us came to Jesus Christ without something in our past we regretted? The point is, as the Bible puts it, all things hidden become known. If there was something in my daughter's past along those lines that hadn't been disclosed before, this would be the time for it. The more they know about each other before they are married, the less chance the enemy has to divide them after they are married.

6. Divine Destiny.

I make certain they discuss their spiritual gifts and callings. If he is called to be a missionary in China and she is called and desires to teach in her home town, with absolutely no desire to travel, they may not be right for each other. If she wants to pursue a career and maybe just have one child much later, but he wants five children right away, maybe that's a deal-breaker. This is where they take an honest look at their divine destinies, deep desires, in addition to personal likes and dislikes, and pray about them. If the Lord brought them together for marriage, then He will show them how to put their gifts and callings together. (You can see the "Toolbox" for the "Gifts" test we use and the "Prepare" questionnaire that helps the couple recognize their level of agreement or disagreement on hundreds of practical questions about preferences and expectations in the marriage. The results of the test expose areas of expectations where the couple needs to sit down and dialog more before marriage).

Step Seven forces "Jumpers" either to step up to the plate and become totally transparent or to run for the hills. Linda and I know that any young man or woman who embraces Step Seven and goes through the entire process of getting all the facts about their life on the table proves their basic good character and integrity of soul. We also understand that they need to see our daughter going through the exact same process of healing of the heart, deliverance, and transparency in all areas. All three of our daughters told us, "I'm so grateful you asked us to do this. I think every couple who wants to get married needs to do this."

During this process, our daughter and the young man find out everything about each other. It is probably possible to hide vital information from each other during the casual and committed dating steps, but in Step Seven there are no more secrets! They are far enough along in the process that they have to come face to face with the truth about themselves and each other, and they have to deal with it. If what they discover is too much for them to handle or kills the romance, then it is a good thing they found out before they got engaged or married.

After they have gone through this process of discipleship and disclosure, I ask them, "Now that you've done everything we have asked, how do you feel about your relationship? Do you feel good? Do you love each other more now than you did before, or do you feel like it's less? Do you like each other more or less? Do you like what you see in a future together? Do you still want to get engaged to be married?"

If one or both of them say no, then we help them redefine the relationship. Do they want to stop dating and remain friends? Do they want to go back and get help on some of their issues and keep dating? Do they want to return to Step Six (Committed Dating) while they work on these issues?

We have worked with some couples who have discovered more issues than other couples, so the response varies. We have some go back a level, and with specific help and counseling, some have seen things in their potential spouse and asked to be released, but the overwhelming majority keep moving forward happily, facing their issues together in a healthy, grateful, mature manner.

On a few occasions this part of the process has been emotionally tough, but it is still a great relief for them to find out they are not right for one another and avoid making a terrible mistake. Linda and I remind them how much we love them both, how much God loves them, and that He has a wonderful mate and a great future ahead for them. So they are not without support and can more easily move on with their lives.

The few times we have had to deal with "Jumpers," we have reached out to them and offered help and discipleship, but most refuse. In almost every case we can think of, they have moved very quickly into a new relationship and have been engaged and married quickly outside of any parental or church guidance or accountability. As time has passed, they have proven themselves to be resistant to anyone's help, to being accountable, and are generally proud and independent.

7. Engagement.

If both the young man and our daughter say they still love one another, respect one another, and believe God has brought them together to be married, then I say, "Okay. Young man, you go pray and think about how you want to ask my daughter to marry you. That's your job. Be creative. You know her pretty well by now, and you should be able to come up with something that would mean a lot to her."

I counsel the young man about finding a way to propose that will not just be meaningful and convenient for him but a memory she will cherish for the rest of their lives. I talk about how we have to learn to give gifts others would like and appreciate instead of giving gifts we would like and appreciate ourselves.

Sometimes he goes away for two or three days, sometimes he takes a couple of weeks or months. He may still take my daughter out on dates, but he is figuring out the very best way he can surprise her and give her a breathtaking memory of a marriage proposal. Also, by this time he knows he has Linda's and my full cooperation! There's no uneasiness, there's no wondering, and there's no anxiety. It's all good.

This whole dating outline is an act of love toward your children. You are showing love and care for them in the same way your heavenly Father shows His love and care for you. You have free, twenty-four/seven access to Him, and you have given your children free, twenty-four/seven access to you as their dating coach and confidant. You listen and share your heart openly and honestly with them, night or day, just like the Father does with you. In return, they are secure in sharing their hearts and minds with you. The dating process is exciting and fruitful for everyone.

Chapter 12

What If You've Blown It?

Joel: My daughters have married really good men. They're better men than I was at that age, and I'm happy about that. Most of all they love God, and all three of them are involved in kingdom life and ministry with us. They are courageous men, and they're passionate for God. They've told all of their friends about "The Talk" and the dating outline I just shared with you. And many of their friends have come to me and said, "Would you have "The Talk" with me?"

Every so often, after I give these young men "The Talk," some of them cry. They say, "I've never had a father that really cared about me like this. I've never had a man talk to me like this. When you share these things with me it scares me! I've never been challenged to grow this much and this fast. I've never been called by anyone to this level of dedication to God, to this level of discipleship and surrender to the Holy Spirit, but somehow I know you care about me - I can feel it. And the plan is clear to me. I can easily understand why it is so good and so powerful. But I've really blown it. I've been in church, but I haven't acted like a Christian."

Some of these young men come under such conviction from the Holy Spirit, that if they aren't saved already, they get saved! If they haven't fully surrendered their lives to the Lordship of Jesus, they do it. They begin telling me how they have hope, but they have blown it so badly that they wonder if they can really have the happiness and joy they see in my family.

At this point, I tell them my own testimony. I was a hypocrite and a rebel towards anything that had to do with God. I was in church but I lived a sinful life, not caring about anyone but myself. I hurt others and caused trouble for many people. But then Jesus forgave me and cleansed me and restored purity and innocence to me. He gave me Linda, and then He gave me three beautiful daughters. If He wanted to do that for me, He wants to do the same thing for them. Restoration and renewal is God's specialty.

Instinctively, these young men know I am telling them the truth. They know someone who loves them unconditionally is showing them the way to live a good life, and the first step is trusting their loving, heavenly Father with their whole life.

Many of the young men I have had "The Talk" with have been solid Christians, but admitted they were afraid to date because it was like driving with no road-map. They didn't know where they were going, and they didn't know what they were supposed to do. As a result, they blew it in the past. This is why "The Talk" is so popular, and all kinds of young men have asked me, "Would you be my spiritual father?" They crave godly fathering and instruction.

The young women who have come to us are no different. More often than not, they have also spent years drifting in the dating scene, getting their hearts broken, often doing things they never set out to do. What we have found is that age doesn't seem to be a factor in blowing it – there has been even a number of young teenage girls who have "experienced it all," and the dating outline is often their only hope that their future might be different from their past.

As these young men and women soon find out, following the dating outline that God gave Linda and me is the answer to their prayers, and their lives are different as they follow it. We strongly encourage them not to wait until they are ready for Step Seven to take the inner healing classes, because as they submit to God's truth in these classes, they allow Him to start a pathway of discipleship and growth that will change them inside, and as He does this, they see the outside of their lives change for the better too.

We tell them that the classes and steps in the outline are practical discipleship steps for any believer: "Start now, no matter what anyone else is doing." We let them know that the key to finding a good mate is to become one. "You run into the right people when you are on the right pathway."

One of our daughters did this. She hadn't blown it in her dating relationships but she recognized she still had some problems she wanted to see changed. She felt hurt and rejected and confused because of some of the experiences that had happened in her life. Finally, she went through the "Healing Week," we ask people to go through in the "Prepare" stage. After that everything changed. Literally everything! She understood God's love for her on a deeper, more personal level. She also understood herself better and who she really was and she got more healed up. As a result, her very next dating experience was entirely different.

The transformation of a young person's life is a wonderful miracle to watch and be a part of. The Father's love, is not just about you receiving the Father's love, it's about you receiving it on deeper levels and learning to give it away. There's the key right there! That is what will change the next generation.

In one generation, both Linda's family and my family went from total destruction and dysfunction to being a loving, happy family. This didn't happen because we are so clever or upstanding; rather it happened simply because we chose to walk in the Father's love and truth instead of our old habits and ideas. Now we are passing on what we have learned and what we experienced to others.

The Father's love and truth are so powerful! They are more powerful than sin, more powerful than rebellion, and nothing the enemy, or the world, or our flesh can throw at us is any match for God's love and truth! That is why Linda and I can confidently declare that no matter how badly you or your kids have blown it, you can begin right now to change your lives, change your family, and powerfully touch the lives of everyone you know.

Merely pray and ask the Holy Spirit to comfort you, to heal you, and to help you forgive yourself and those who have hurt you. Then ask Him to show you how to use this dating outline to set things right in your family. Maybe you are widowed or divorced and starting to date again yourself, maybe you are a teenager like I was, and you've been promiscuous and have just been drifting through life like you had a sign on your back, saying, "Hurt me.

Abuse me. Reject me. Cause me pain. Show me how to mess up my life," or maybe you are a parent or a grandparent and all the influences of the world we live in are really scaring you for your children and grandchildren. It doesn't matter where you are in life, how old you are, or how you or your family members have blown it in the past. God tells us that His mercies are new every morning. That means today is a brand-new day, and you can start fresh. You can get healed and restored to purity, you can get clean and re-established with your divine destiny, and your relationships can be renewed and repaired as well.

Our Father has made it so simple! All you have to do is ask for His forgiveness. Next, receive His love and chose to love and forgive yourself. By doing this, you will be able to freely love and forgive others. You will be able to allow Him to fully restore your family's destiny and help your son or your daughter find God's mate for them.

The truth is you don't have to be in a panic during the dating years - you can actually enjoy them. The Father will help you be the best coach you can be, and then your team will win! Through His love and wisdom, you can see your family transformed in just one generation, just like we did.

Chapter 13

What About Your Church?

Joel and Linda: Maybe you have read this book, adapted the dating outline to your family, and it worked so beautifully that you want every family in your church to experience the benefits of it. We suggest going to see your pastor and/or the head of counseling in your church and giving them a copy of the book.

Tell your pastor or head of counseling how the dating outline has benefited you and your kids. Ask them to prayerfully read the book and consider training dating coaches, perhaps mature couples who have successful marriages themselves, or older single believers who have a reputation for living integrous and pure lives.

When you read the testimonies in Chapter 16, you will see for yourself how young people and adults alike are crying out for help with their lives, especially when it comes to dating and finding a mate. The world has nothing to offer them but deception, the destruction of their souls, and sometimes the degradation of their bodies.

Many of our young people have already experienced this downward spiral, and many of the kids in our churches are now old enough to understand that it will be a miracle if they can stay pure for marriage and marry the right person.

Kids look around them and see their parents or other kids' parents getting divorced. They watch the older kids saying and doing things they instinctively know are not right, but everyone is doing it, right? They hear one way to live in church, but see another way of living at school, on TV, in books, at home, and the list goes on. They begin to have a hard time discerning who is right and who is wrong. They begin to question if what they are being taught at church and in their home is practical in the world they live in.

Too often, the church doesn't address the questions our children and youth have with practical "How To" help. As a result, we see so many church kids fall into terrible sin and get trapped in it at an early age. As fathers and mothers in the church, we must take the lead and offer them a practical but fun alternative, not just empty words. We can do this with confidence because God and His Word are on our side. We are the ones with the truth!

Maybe you have read this book and you are a pastor. You see the benefits of the dating outline for families, and you are already thinking of particular couples and single people in your congregation who would be great at being dating coaches. Perhaps you know of some great business-people who would love to share their wisdom with young people. Maybe you even know of (or already have) a good communications class they could take.

The only thing that is holding you back is that you are wondering about the inner healing stuff we require in Step Seven. We encourage you to contact Restoring the Foundations (RTF) and go through their "Healing Week." We believe it's for everyone. See for yourself what we, and all the testimonies in this book, are talking about … changed lives!

Once you see the incredible value of a "Healing Week," please share it with everyone you know. Invite a team from RTF to your church and host a "Healing Week" for those who are interested. Then RTF will train you and/or a team from your congregation, to do the "Healing Week" in your church. We promise you, it will be one of the best things you have ever done for yourself, for your congregation, and for all the young people who are wondering who they are and how to live their lives.

We have written So You Want to Date My Daughter?!!! not only to help parents who are wondering what to do with their kids during the dating years, but also to give the Body of Christ a powerful, strategic weapon to turn a perverse generation into a righteous generation.

The enemy has always known that if he can turn the young to evil thinking and perverse ways, he can rule the nation and the world when their generation comes to maturity. Well, guess what? Our Father knows what the devil is up to and He has given us strategies and plans that will overthrow any destructive plan the devil has against us and our children!

One of the most horrible things the devil has done to our kids is to twist their minds and give them lies about innocence and sexual purity. He has done this in all forms of media, from magazines and books to movies, television, and the internet. This is why the dating outline is such a powerful weapon - it is why young men and women instinctively know the power of it and are drawn to it.

When kids and young people understand the freedom and joy of a sexually pure and virtuous life, they will run with it. They love a righteous cause and there is nothing more righteous than remaining pure in heart and body for God and for their mate. Furthermore, when they become leaders, the enemy will have lost his grip on their generation and God's love and truth will reign on the earth through them.

We do not see this book as just a tool to help families, although that in itself is a great thing. We know the dating outline is like an intercontinental ballistic missile given from God to destroy the lies of the enemy with His truth and love. These simple steps can change the world, one family at a time, one church at a time, one community at a time, and one nation at a time. All glory, honor and praise to Jesus, the fiery bridegroom of us all!

Chapter 14

Quick Reference
(To the Dating Outline)

Joel and Linda: Following is an abbreviated, easy reference to the dating outline we've just discussed in detail. When you are coaching a couple in their dating and want to determine what's next - when this or that happens, etc., this Quick Reference will help. It is also the outline we use after "The Talk," when a couple announces their desire to date each other. What we have noticed is that every time a couple wants to go to the next level in courtship, they can't remember, and we can't always recall either, all the opportunities and requirements of each sequential level, so we pull out the Quick Reference and have a brief meeting regarding the objectives and requirements of the next level. It's quick and easy, and you don't have to thumb through all the pages of this book to find out what is next.

Dating Outline Quick Reference

1. The Spirit of Adulthood — Rite of Passage

    a. Celebrate entrance into adulthood by taking your son or daughter on their first date.

    b. Begin with the end in mind: "What do you want your wedding day to look like?

Would you like to wear white? Would you like to be a virgin on that day? What kind of person do you want to be on that day?"

c. Give them a ring, symbolizing the covenant of innocence and purity you have made with them.

d. Go through the "Rite of Passage — No Regrets" program with your child. Lay hands on your child and release "the blessing" from mom and dad and the generational legacy.

2. The Spirit of Friendship

   a. Level #1: Pre-dating

      a. Casual events as friends.

      b. Group dating as friends.

      c. No commitment to being boyfriend or girlfriend with anyone yet.

      d. Monitor levels of obedience, responsibility, observance of curfews, attitudes, etc.

    b.   Level #2: Casual Dating

          a.   "The Talk" – (The "car" analogy - ("If I were to borrow it …")

          b.   Cover the boundaries ("Anything you are uncomfortable to do with me …")

          c.   Covenant of Innocence and Purity: Invite the couple into the covenant you have with your daughter. Make a commitment to purity.

          d.   Psalm 133: How good and pleasant it is when we live in unity in our families! Invite the young couple to honor the family and its individuals and values during dating.

3.   The Spirit of Courtship — Level #3: Committed Dating

    a.   Learn about each other.

    b.   Enjoy good, clean dates and events.

    c.   Be transparent and observant.

d. Maintain and honor existing friendships and relationships outside of the dating relationship.

    i. Watch out for inappropriate possessiveness, a spirit of control or jealousy.

    ii. Develop a life and relationships that include healthy friendships with others. Don't fixate on the dating relationship at the cost of other relationships.

4. The Spirit of Preparation — Level #4: Serious Dating

    a. The Power of Purity:

        i. Serious dating includes a renewed call to the power of purity. The goal is to focus on Jesus and see what He wants to show you in this important season of your life about your own destiny preparedness.

        ii. The call to purity is not just a call to chastity or birth control. Rather, it is a call to what Jesus promised: "Blessed are the pure in heart, for they will see God" (Matthew 5:8). Jesus is going to open your eyes to many things in this season.

b.   Provision:

   i.   Purity and innocence will not provide us with a revelation of God, it will align us with God's supernatural provision for a man and woman who are seriously dating, or who are looking ahead to the possibility of becoming a family in covenant with God.

   ii.   You will begin to "see" God's love and God's provision manifesting in a powerful way toward your finances, home and employment. When a dating couple maintains sexual purity in their relationship instead of confusion, there is a growing clarity about their future together and a

faith that God will provide in every
area.

c. Purpose:

    i. Purity and innocence help reveal
your purpose and passion and give
you the courage to fulfill your life's
calling. This is essential to dating
with destiny in mind. Impurity and a
guilty conscience sap your
confidence, your clarity in hearing
God and understanding God's will
for your life. Our goal is to lift our
gaze upward – above our immediate
preoccupations and above our
longings for human companionship
to the Maker who created us for
Himself.

    ii. Assignments:

        a. Commit to personal purity as a
lifestyle.

        b. Men: Read *"Every Man's Battle"*
by Fred Stoeker.

c. Women: Read "*Passion and Purity*" by Elizabeth Elliot.

d. Preparation – "Boot Camp":

Serious dating includes a call to "boot camp" for those individuals who think they may want to enter into marriage some day.

If a person admits that they want to be in a healthy marriage someday, they must make a commitment to the Lord to participate wholeheartedly to a pathway of personal development, spiritual growth, and the healing of life's hurts. The motivation is to become a person who is good marriage material, not just a person who is in love and looking for someone to meet their needs.

Just like you would not send a soldier into war without basic training or boot camp for preparation, young men and women should never be sent into the spiritual warfare surrounding marriage without a "boot camp" experience.

Personal Discipleship at this level includes:

I.   Breaking Free Classes – Part I & II (see the "Toolbox" page).

II. Restoring The Foundations – "Healing Week" (see the "Toolbox" page).

III. Healing of the Heart Class – Part I & II (see the "Toolbox" page).
     [*Note*: Every person who desires to be a healthy, healed up disciple of Jesus should take these classes, regardless of their desire to be married.]

5. The Spirit of Pre-Engagement — Level #5: Pre-Engagement (Pre-Engagement/Prepare Stage)

After completing the four discipleship classes listed above, if the couple still desire their relationship to go to the next level, they are most likely considering engagement and marriage.

Before getting engaged, we have discovered it is best to complete the level we call Pre-engagement and Prepare Stage.

a. Qualifying Tests:
    i. Credit report
    ii. Blood tests
    iii. Physical exams.
    iv. Current budget review
    v. Financial review
    vi. Personality and Gifts Tests (see the "Toolbox" page)
    vii. Spiritual Gifts Test
    viii. D.I.S.C. Test/Profile
    ix. Taylor Johnson Temperament Test
    x. Prepare and Enrich Test (Differences Inventory).
b. Couples Communication Class (see the "Toolbox" page for information).
c. Pre-Marital Class – "Saving Your Marriage Before It Starts" (see the "Toolbox" page).
d. Parents' Blessing
    i. Ask parents on both sides of the family for their blessing to get engaged.

ii.   Figure out how you want to answer the question when people ask "When's the wedding date?"

e.   Give the man the assignment of prayerfully considering how he wants to ask his bride for her hand in marriage. Tell him to "Go and ask God for wisdom and creativity. Believe God cares and will give you wisdom and creativity on how to build a romantic memory for her."

6.   The Spirit of Covenant — Level #6: Engagement

    a.   How, when and where do you want to make a public announcement of your engagement? (With each of our sons-in-law, they surprised the girls when and how they asked them to be their wife. Then the men brought them to our house for a surprise celebration party where many of their friends were waiting... like a birthday party. We also had communion at the house and prayers of blessing by the parents at the party. We also had their engagement announced at church).

b. Make wedding plans

c. The Budget for the wedding:

   i. What is the budget?

d. Wedding event plans.

   i. Outline of things to be done, including by whom and what deadlines.

e. Honeymoon plans:

   i. What is the budget?

   ii. What do you want to do?

f. Personal Coaching:

   a. "The Total Man" – To help the man become sensitive and thoughtful in the area of marital sex on the honeymoon and beyond (See the "Toolbox" page).

   b. Men – "The Best Sex of Your Life" (DVD) (see the "Toolbox" page).

   c. Both read "Getting Your Sex Life Off to a Good Start" (see the "Toolbox" page).

7. The Spirit of Marriage – Level #7: Bonding and Blessing

   a. Receiving your new "son" or "daughter" into your family and your heart.

      i. Ask for the "Spirit of Adoption". God's love and grace for your new family member.

      ii. Make the decision and effort to show affection to, as well as and communicate meaningfully, to your new family member.

   b. What do you want to call this new member of the family? ("son"/"daughter")? What do they want to call you ("mom"/"dad")?

   c. The call and commitment to pray daily for your new son and daughter, now more than ever.

A note from Joel: When our first daughter was about to get married, many of our friends began to ask me, "How do you feel about giving your daughter away?" I told them that I was excited, like I had reached a goal. I also remember saying several times "my part is done." I was speaking "out of the abundance of my heart" and I was wrong (Matthew 12:34). I didn't realize how short-sighted and shallow this attitude was until I had a vivid dream from the Lord just a few weeks before the wedding. In the dream, the Lord confronted my sloppy attitude about being "done" and he made it clear to me how essential it would be for my adult children to have my continual, daily-prayer support so they could reach their destinies. I had woefully underestimated several key things: First, the level of hatred the devil has for marriage, family and godly grandchildren. He is viciously afraid of godly heritage, generational legacies as well as generational anointings and blessings being passed on and growing.

The devil is also afraid of the breaking of sin patterns especially pertaining to "the sins of the fathers being visited upon the third and fourth generation" (Deuteronomy 5:9). Satan is a legalist and he knows that he has a legal right to attack the future generations as long as the fathers in each generation keep coming into agreement with him by yielding to the same sin patterns as the previous generations. But when someone, like me, decides it's time to break the patterns, resist the devil, repent for the sins of my fathers, and directly apply the blood of Jesus to the generational iniquities in order to break generational patterns and curses, Satan begins to lose the legal rights he has enjoyed for generations.

In other words, things begin to get better and better from generation to generation. We start tapping into the generational blessings on a whole new level in which God promises to "visit," bless, and "show mercy to thousands" of generations of those who love Him and obey (Exodus 20:6).

The point is this: when my kids get married, I'm not done praying, blessing and encouraging them. The warfare against my family line and generational legacy is not over. The blessings have just begun! My job and my influence as "father" does not end at the wedding altar. It transitions and goes up a notch if I will take my place appropriately.

When I woke up from the dream, I was shaken. The first thing I did was sincerely and deeply repented for excusing myself from the key position I had been given in the cosmic conflict over God's commitment to release His blessings on our children and over our children's children. Then I asked for wisdom and discernment so I would know how to fulfill my role. Next, I committed myself to pray daily in the Spirit for my daughter, my new son, and their family, home, and destiny. I accepted my calling as a spiritual patriarch and accepted the spiritual authority that goes with that calling. I was reminded of the words of the Apostle Paul where he committed himself to be a spiritual father to those in his life: "You have a thousand teachers but not many Fathers" (1 Corinthians 4:15). It doesn't mean I stick my nose in where I'm not wanted - it means I continue to serve (often behind the scenes) as a spiritual-support, prayer-covering, spiritual-shield and intercessor. For my children and for my legacy, I am a spiritual warrior with spiritual authority who will "wrestle" in the invisible realms. On the outside I show them love, I bless them, and I encourage, hug, and kiss "my kids." But in the unseen, when I serve them in this way, it is amazing how often they call for advice, ask questions, come over to our house to share their dreams, visions, and challenges. They call us for prayer support, asking us to agree in prayer for that new house, that problem at work, that change in the job, that promotion, that sickness, that pregnancy, etc. It's all very natural and "normal" for them, and for us as mom and dad, to share life on this new level.

That's Level Seven: "Bonding and Blessing." We don't have any grandchildren yet but I believe that will be another level of influence if I wisely take my place to bond with and bless those future grandchildren. I remember how my heart was wide open and how I revered and respected my grandparents. I longed for their affection, direction, confirmation and blessing. Unfortunately, they did not realize what a great opportunity of influence they could have had in my tender heart. Grandparents have the potential to make a lasting spiritual and emotional impact if they use every opportunity and their spiritual authority wisely.

Now the dating season has passed and all my girls are married, I see how shallow and foolish I was to think and say "I'm done," just because I was done with the outline and was preparing to walk my daughter down the aisle to "give her away." Time and experience has proven I'm not "done" - I'm just starting over on a brand new level!

Chapter 15

A Little Advice

Joel and Linda: We suggest parents begin the first few steps of this outline at least by the time your child starts junior high, even if they are homeschooled. As we have been privileged to teach seminars on this dating outline in various places, one question that is often asked by parents is, "How old do you think children should be before I start using this outline? At what age do we take them through the various steps?"

We know kids vary in their developmental stages and ages; however, if you ask effective Christian leaders, whose occupation is to work with children and teens from "normal" Christian homes, they will tell you there is very little difference between when Christian and non-Christian kids need guidance, information, leadership, and direction concerning human growth and development, hormones, sexual curiosity, interest in the opposite sex, and sexual desire. Also, competent Christian leaders will tell you it is common for all kids to become curious about what is happening to them and their bodies, especially when they know things are changing. When their questions are left unanswered and their hormones are not appropriately addressed, they often become experimental and/or sexually active to one degree or another, typically beginning during the junior high years. Unwittingly, this is when many young teens begin to build habits and adopt behaviors that lead to impurity, bondage, guilt, and shame.

Something we sense Christian parents do not want to hear or believe, but there is concrete evidence to support what we are presenting to you in this book, is that there is no perceptible difference in the level of interest between Christian and non-Christian kids at this age. Their hormones and the physical changes they are experiencing are forcing these issues and questions on them, no matter how innocent and protected they have been. We need to stop kidding ourselves and meet the challenge head-on and embrace the opportunity we have been given to provide godly training. The difference is not in our kids' inclinations, but in the way we prepare them for the approaching transitions and seasons.

Christian youth experts tell us that the more strict, protective, and non-communicative parents are about these issues, the more likely the child will be to not grasp the truth about concerning their bodies or to willingly receive the godly help and guidance they desperately need. In other words, children raised in strict, protective homes are more likely to not get the answers they need and to feel tempted to search for information through experimentation about sex from outside sources, including friends, internet, school sex education programs, and other places that are probably giving out mixed or unscriptural advice.

We believe the most important advice we can give you is to tackle these issues with your child the moment the Holy Spirit says, "Now!" Follow the dating outline, take advantage of the classes and programs available to you in the "Toolbox" section of the book, and listen to the Father's prompting to ensure that your child will not perish because of lack of knowledge (Hosea 4:6). Use these steps and resources to firmly establish your role as your child's loving and trustworthy life coach and dating coach before their hormones even begin to show up or the world has any time to lead them astray.

First dates have less to do with specific ages as they have to do with a healthy relationship between the parent/coach and the child. Take every opportunity to make sure you and your child are on the same page, of the same mind, walking in the spirit of love and unity, and working towards the same goals. If you have relationship problems or communication misunder-standings when they are in elementary school, don't expect it to get better later on. Instead, begin working on these issues of discipline and communication early so you can avoid terrible catastrophes later. (See the "Toolbox" for the books "How To Really Love Your Child," "How To Really Love Your Teenager," and "Discipline With Love and Logic.")

One of the ways you can build a great relationship of love and trust with your child is to be transparent and honest with them whenever they ask questions. The Holy Spirit will always give you the right answer. If you don't know what to say, just respond with "That's a great question! Let me think about the best way to answer you and I'll get back to you very soon with what I believe is the right answer." Then, go ask God for wisdom and believe that He will give it to you. Listen and look for the godly answer - you'll find it. When you go back to them with the wisdom, they will be grateful. There's no need to be upset or frightened if they ask you a question which you think is not "age appropriate." What is age appropriate to you may not be what the Holy Spirit knows is age appropriate for your child - He will tell you what to say either way.

It is also important to set good, biblical ground-rules regarding attitudes and obedience so that when they are older and ready to date, they will have a solid trust in your ability to provide the security they need to successfully date with destiny in mind. Have they been trained to keep boundaries and curfews as they attend group events and group dates? Have they preformed well with an attitude and spirit of unity and maturity during these events and dates? The answer to these questions will let both you and your child know if they are ready to go to the next level and have their first date.

Every level and season of the dating outline provides you with mile-markers of maturity and growth that let you know if your young son or daughter is ready to go to the next level. In the meantime, our best advice in using the dating outline is to be a growing person yourself in getting your own heart healed up, learning parenting skills, taking time to enjoy God's Word, praying without ceasing, listening to the Holy Spirit and doing what the Word and the Spirit tell you to do!

Chapter 16

Testimonies That Prove
the Dating Outline Works!

Marion

I really appreciated the opportunity to sit down and discuss expectations and necessities for both me and my lady with someone who was a father figure to us both and who had been there before. Driving her home after our first experience with the pastors' dating outline, Sarah said "I didn't know so much was involved in what you have to do!" I felt a huge sense of relief - I didn't feel like I had to bear the burden of moving our relationship forward by myself. I felt completely relaxed and liberated by being able to pinpoint where our relationship was at the time, where we wanted it to go, and what our individual expectations were. Men and women are different enough that we don't need the added mystique of popular cultural dating norms. Sure, it's fun to wonder what's going on in the other person's head when you're dating - it can seem exciting and romantic, but it is way better to know what the other person thinks and expects and to be able to move forward together.

Now we're engaged to be married and couldn't be happier because we got here together.

I would definitely recommend this system to couples and singles who are interested in building a relationship that is designed from the start to last forever. I have seen it work for some of my friends, but the real proof is in my own experience and the fact that my relationship is stronger now than it has ever been before. We're excited about spending the rest of our lives together as best friends and as a team.

I also recommend that each member of a relationship use the time of singleness and dating for prayerful self-exploration and relational intercession. This will give a person perspective into how best to relate to others and foster righteous bonds. Sowing into relationships with friends, families, and even enemies will bring a harvest of healthy relational-identity and help foster Christ-like romance within a dating relationship.

Sarah

One of the most helpful things about going through the dating outline was having a mentor with wisdom and experience who was able to affirm us and say, "It looks like you're ready to move forward." Our culture is severely lacking in true fathers and mothers. There are many people who will advise you out of impure motives or who can only give advice that is motivated out of their own hurt. Having guidance from people who have taken the time to get their hearts healed up and who only want to see you walk into your destiny is a rare thing these days.

The most noticeable effect the dating outline had on us was the confidence that came to our relationship in knowing that we were on the same page and being prepared together for a healthy future. Having some direction removed a lot of the confusion that we had experienced concerning each other's expectations for the relationship and its various seasons.

I would definitely recommend this approach to other couples, parents, and mentors. I felt like we were some of the most blessed people on the planet to be given such a healthy start in our life together.

Shane

What I liked about the dating outline was that I was able to really get to know the person I was about to marry. It was tough at times, but I think everything was needed. The dating outline made it easier to talk about all issues, and it really kept me from making any wrong decisions.

Cristin

My experience with the dating outline has been a good one. Up until I really submitted myself to it, my story consisted of heartbreak after heartbreak. My past seasons of dating with boys had been good, and for the most part had been healthy, but each experience seemed to steal a piece of my heart and leave me feeling a little more rejected and a little more broken than before.

I attempted to go through the dating outline with one boyfriend after another. At some point or another, the boyfriend would try to push things along, hurdle over benchmarks, or propose alternative solutions to this method of dating. Consequently, those relationships didn't last long.

Finally, after going through a Healing Week and beginning to take the dating outline really seriously, my perspective changed. No longer did I view myself as rejected, unloved, or have the innate desire to control others, my relationships, or even my future. Instead, I embraced God's timing and had peace concerning His ultimate plan for my life and my future husband, whoever he would be.

Shortly after this, Mr. Right found me and I was swept off my feet! The entire dating experience felt so right, so real, and so romantic. I never knew that dating could be so easy, let alone falling in love!

While the process seemed tedious and time-consuming, I would have to emphatically assure others that for every step, every season, and every issue God decides to put His finger on, it is all worth it! Not only was I prepared for the details that come with marriage (finances, solving disagreements, etc.), but I had a good perspective and understanding of myself, my husband, and my marriage. I had more self-esteem and an understanding of my call in life as a wife, as an individual, and someday as a mother. I also had a greater revelation of what it means to love and to be loved, as well as what it means to be the Bride of Christ.

I would highly recommend this approach to other couples, parents, mentors, pastors, and churches. And I would add that it's not necessary to wait to do all the inner healing classes until you think you found "the one." Begin the process now, as a Bride in love with Jesus, and see what happens as He reveals the Father's heart to you. You will find yourself changing and becoming more like the person God created you to be, a person of God's love and character, free from blame and shame, stepping into your divine destiny.

Chad

I liked the accountability, as well as the ability to not feel rushed or pressured to go at a certain speed, when dating someone. There was an ease about the dating experience that I hadn't ever experienced before. Without the physical relationship, you can move as slow or as fast as you want.

There was nothing about the dating outline that I didn't like or would change. It was laid out very nicely and I would recommend this to dating couples, as well as parents of kids who are dating, because the outline is very specific on how the dating experience will go - it addresses most questions before you get involved with someone, allowing all pressure to be eliminated.

Kelsey

The dating outline was a different approach to dating than I had ever experienced, considered, or had even known about. The steps are so clearly laid out, so it wasn't hard or overwhelming. It really took the pressure off of trying to figure out what was going on in the other person's mind.

Because of the clear steps, we were both always on the same page, and couldn't move to the next level until we both were ready. I never had to have that conversation in my head, asking myself, "Is he ready to propose or does he just want to be friends?" because I already knew!

Pastors Joel and Linda made it really easy for us. It was very relaxing, and it was ultimately up to us how fast or how slow we wanted to take our relationship. We found that the more we progressed in the steps, the deeper our relationship developed and grew.

Our relationship felt really good and clean, easy and fun. It really does take the stress out of dating because we didn't have to focus on anything except getting to know one another better and deciding if this person was worth investing more time in.

I just wish I would have had this a long time ago. I could have saved a lot of guys the heartbreak they would experience from the outcome of dating me, and, of course, I could have saved myself some heartache a couple of times too. This dating outline saved me.

One thing that I liked was that I could walk away from the developing relationship at any point with no strings attached if I wanted, and it would be okay. Plus, I didn't have to invest any more of myself than the other person was willing to invest of himself … so, why wouldn't I try it? There's nothing I had to lose!

My testimony is that it worked for me, and it was exactly what I needed. Through the whole process, there are things we did during each step to prepare ourselves and get ourselves cleaned up for the next step and for the prospect that marriage could be the result of all this preparation. I got really cleaned up through the classes I took at the church and got rid of a lot of the junk (soul-ties from past relationships, ungodly beliefs that I had about relationships and about myself, fear, etc.).

It's really amazing what God can do if you let Him, and it's really amazing what He will do if you both put Him at the center of your relationship from beginning to end. He will protect you and He will prepare you.

Another amazing and wonderful thing that I discovered (now that I'm married and have spoken with other married couples) is that because of the things you do in preparing yourself and one another during each step, there is no surprise after you get married! There's no, "Oh, did I mention that I'm $75,000 in debt?" or "I have a gambling problem?" or "This is totally different than my last marriage!" or "I have a phobia of taking out the trash and picking up after myself." Yikes!

When Pastors Joel and Linda say that this outline will help you to do everything that you can possibly do to prepare yourself for the "I dos" and the "happily ever after," it's really true! I'm so thankful that the Budds shared this with Chad and me. We got married one year and one week to the day that we embarked upon the dating journey and it has been so fun!!!

Chris

When I began the dating outline out of my desire to date one of the Pastors' daughters, I thought the rules were absolutely absurd. There were certain ways I did things, but I quickly realized that it was not going to pan out the way I had planned!

I had a big problem with doing Steps Six and Seven before we could even get engaged. I understood the purpose of going through these steps before we got married but not before we could get engaged. I felt that after all the hoops I had been through, that should be at least one thing I got to decide. I felt that they were unrealistic goals leading to unrealistic results.

Now that I am at the end of the steps I can look back and realize that there are many benefits to all the classes and personality tests we took, and that it is something that I can take pride in. This daughter is now my wife and I worked very hard for her! Now I feel that I deserve her and our life together will improve tremendously!

Marriage is a license and, like any license, there are tests and evaluations that one must go through in order to pass. Somewhere along the way people have forgotten the importance of taking steps before their marriage begins. I wouldn't expect the young man who comes to take your daughter out to understand the benefits of what you're going to ask of him, but he will after he's completed the tasks. I have and now I understand.

Haley

I liked that the dating outline encouraged a man to work hard for me, for our future, and for our marriage. It also taught us both a lot, mainly things we knew but were not sure of how to go about. We are both proud to say now that we have never worked harder for a successful relationship.

We both lived an hour and a half away from the church that offered all the classes, and this made the process difficult and lengthy. After doing the "Healing Week," however, we had a lot easier time getting along with our families and with each other. We found a few things we had not discussed that needed to be talked about, and the classes also allowed us to see each other in a new light, revealing our strengths, weaknesses, personality flaws, and even positive mannerisms.

I would definitely recommend the dating outline to other young couples, newly married or about to be married, or couples that are having a hard time in their marriage. The best way for me to describe this whole experience is that it seems like a long journey, but it is very beneficial in the end.

Isaac

I liked the way the steps were laid out so clearly. The dating outline helped to break down each stage so we were able to focus on the season of the relationship we were in as opposed to looking at the sometimes distracting big picture. Overall it was great and I would do it again.

The dating outline gave a "regrouping" point, a place we could start when evaluating our relationship as concerns or problems arose - it allowed us to get on the same page quickly. The approach also encourages growth as individuals as well as a couple. Instead of our focus being, "Are we getting married?" it has been, "Are we growing?"

I felt like this outline put the focus on enjoying each other and the Lord in the relationship process as opposed to "figuring it out." This difference has allowed both of us to grow more than we would have using the approaches we had seen until this point.

Kara

I liked that Pastor Joel and Pastor Linda took time to explain the different levels of dating to us and the basic principles of dating and relationships. I always felt very clear as to where we were going and what we were doing as a couple after meeting to discuss our progress with the outline.

Having this dating plan took a lot of stress out of our relationship. It has also helped me tremendously in the area of healthy communication. I would recommend doing the dating outline very early in the relationship as to have a clear "plan" and idea of what a healthy relationship looks like from the start.

One of my favorite things about the dating outline is it leaves no room for surprises in the relationship. I love that the plan covered important relational topics that we might not have thought about otherwise. I also really like that our relationship was addressed as a covenant, knowing that we we're anointed for the different levels of dating.

Dave

The dating outline gave me a structure for building a healthy relationship. Like most, I had rules and morals to follow but no direct structure on how to put them together to reach a goal. So for me, having this process of dating laid out was an eye-opening experience and it gave me the confidence that even if things didn't work out I could leave her the way I found her or hopefully better.

I thought hard about whether there would be anything I would change, but as well as it worked for me, I can't imagine what could be changed. My relationship with Joelle (now my wife) was healthy, with great communication from beginning to present. We have moments of learning, as all do, but we don't question each other's hearts because the classes we took, and this dating process, opened us up to each other's truth before we got married.

I had a clear head and a clean conscience. I grew up in the church, but then I had my time in the world. Those in the world, who haven't had the solid upbringing I did, may not have the convictions I had growing up. The hard part about living outside of the truth is actually the truth part. Often, one wants to follow it but there is little to grab hold of to help anchor oneself from the societal acceptances of independence and sex outside of marriage.

Anyone who has grown up similar to me and has had their share of attempted Christian (moral) relationships, knows the pain of trying to follow your heart, express your freedom as an adult, stay moral, and not be a boring prude. This dating outline, once committed to by both people, makes all that so much simpler.

Couples don't know everything. We need help. Relationship is the container that holds the most powerful force inside and outside of time and space: the love of God. So, far be it from us to try to build a structure strong enough to hold this tangible power, as well as take on the stewardship of another human being's heart and spirit, without help from the One who designed marriage. Pastors Joel and Linda are not God, but they do have His wisdom, and the dating outline they have received from Him is biblical.

Also, parents also don't know everything and need help. I don't know what parent wouldn't want to protect their child from the subtle acceptances that are creeping into our society. This relationship-building structure is a pretty good example of that strong tower that the righteous run into and are safe.

Joelle

The dating outline gave us a goal, something to look forward to, something to work towards together. During the process, it could be said that it is also self-improvement time - you get to see things about yourself you never knew were there. In a way, it's like insurance because you know everything will be okay in the end - because it's an agreement with a positive outcome. There is a plan in place for everyone involved and it brings trust because it makes you want to be honest. It takes the pressure off because no one is guessing where this thing, called a relationship, is going.

I don't think there is anything that can be changed! The dating outline gives as much freedom for fast or slow movement as you want. Anyone who can't follow it, in my opinion, has issues they need to deal with. It's easy, it's clear, and it's strict. If you care about you, your relationship, your partner, and your future, you shouldn't have any problem sticking to it.

There was a tremendous amount of honesty and freedom. That's what the entire thing is about - honesty and communicating it. It was fun because we had a common goal and there wasn't any guesswork involved. The outline was presented at the very beginning, so we knew what the process was supposed to look like. We were able to be ourselves from the beginning instead of trying to make something happen.

I would recommend the dating outline because the examples of relationships today have been perverted and you can't tell what it's supposed to be like. I know a lot of younger people who have said they never want to get married because they have never seen a marriage that works. So now they are going to just "have fun."

Another reason I would recommend the dating outline is because it encourages growth and maturity, and most relationships I know are lacking that very thing. It also brings a sense of accomplishment. This thing isn't easy, but if you do it, you will feel rewarded the whole way through.

Jennifer

My fiancé and I decided to take the pastors' recommendations to heart and slow down our engagement process to fill in the stages we had missed. For example, we knew shortly after we met that we would be getting married, but this revelation didn't give us reason to miss the blessings of going through the dating outline, especially when the Lord had provided through our church the opportunity to improve our relationship through cycles of inner healing and deliverance.

Actually, we almost did move forward too quickly, but the Lord gave us grace to see that we would better magnify our strengths by waiting for "the fullness of time" to reach our particular situation (Galatians 4:4).

I enjoyed the personalized approach, with the detailed recommendations that gave each couple the wisdom and understanding to choose how high they wanted to go. The "seasons and levels" have given us a valuable roadmap to chart our progress along the journey.

I believe this approach could work for all couples who have willing and teachable hearts, even couples who don't yet know the Lord could benefit from this wisdom. In the future, I could see such a program extending beyond church walls to minister to individuals who are looking for the rewards purity brings, but who don't yet have the revelation that purity is what they seek.

In my experience at a secular private university that brought in a culturally and economically diverse student population, I noticed a trend: most of the students had lost their purity before they graduated (though I could see their hearts were after the mystery, beauty, and passion with which purity colors love) and had stumbled into sheer monotony and dullness as their quest for pleasure left them finding fulfillment nowhere.

I was formerly a part of this trend, but an encounter with the Lord changed my experience entirely, and I can now return to memories of my life at university and see how many people hunger for the revelation of purity in their hearts but are held back out of ignorance or because they cannot tolerate the packaging in which most messages about purity come.

What's unique about the dating outline is its freedom from control. Recommendations are presented in light of the reality that there is no purity outside of the blood of Jesus. Because the focus goes beyond purity to focus on each individual's achieving the highest level of freedom as they walk through courtship, the program makes possible a deeper relationship accountability that lays a strong foundation for each couple to begin a life together. Additionally, I like how the program honors all related parties, including parents and mentors, by establishing them as stakeholders in the welfare and blessing of the couple.

The Tool Box

There are some resources we recommend for use in the dating outline for parents and dating coaches. If any of the books or classes go out of print or become unavailable, we suggest that you consult your local church, pastors or good Christian marriage and family counselors for suggestions on the specific topics in the dating outline.

1. "Rite of Passage – No Regrets!"

> Cristin Hamman
> Open Bible Fellowship
> 1439 E. 71st St.
> Tulsa, OK 74136
> 918-492-5511
> cristinh@obftulsa.org

2. "Healing of the Heart" Classes – Part I & II

> Firestorm School of Ministry
> 1439 E. 71st St.
> Tulsa, OK 74136
> 918-492-5511 x39
> info@obftulsa.org

3. "Breaking Free" Classes – Part I & II

> Firestorm School of Ministry
> 1439 E. 71st St.
> Tulsa, OK 74136
> 918-492-5511 x39

info@obftulsa.org

4. "Effective Communication" Class

Firestorm School of Ministry
1439 E. 71st St.
Tulsa, OK 74136
918-492-5511 x39
info@obftulsa.org

5. "Spiritual Gifts Test"

Open Bible Fellowship
1439 E. 71st St.
Tulsa, OK 74136
seniorpastors@obftulsa.org

6.   DISC Test

Open Bible Fellowship
1439 E. 71st St.
Tulsa, OK 74136
seniorpastors@obftulsa.org

7. "Restoring the Foundations" – "Healing Week"
www.rtfi.org

8. "Prepare and Enrich" Questionnaire

Open Bible Fellowship
1439 E. 71st St.
Tulsa, OK 74136
seniorpastors@obftulsa.org

9. "Saving Your Marriage Before it Starts or Goes Any Further" - Book

     Author: Drs. Les & Leslie Parrott
     Publisher: Zondervan
     www.realrelationships.com

10. For Men – "Every Man's Battle - Book

     Authors: Stephen Arterburn and Fred Stoeker
     Publisher: Random House, Inc.
     www.everymansbattle.com

11. For Women – "Passion and Purity" - Book

     Author: Elisabeth Elliot
     Publisher: Baker Publishing Group
     www.elisabethelliot.org

13. For Engaged Men – "The Total Man" - Book

     Read Chapters 18-21
     Author: Dan Benson
     Publisher: Tyndale House Publishers, Inc.

14. For Engaged Men – "The Best Sex of Your Life"- DVD

     Author: Douglas Weiss
     Heart to Heart Counseling Center
     5080 Mark Dabling Blvd
     Colorado Springs, CO 80918
     719-278-3708
     info@sexaddict.com
     www.sexaddict.com

15.   For Engaged Men and Women – "Getting Your Sex Life Off to a Great Start"

Author: Clifford L. Penner & Joyce J. Penner
Publisher: Thomas Nelson
penners@passionatecommitment.com
www.passionatecommitment.com

About the Authors

Joel and Linda Budd have been the senior pastors of Open Bible Fellowship in Tulsa, Oklahoma, for over 25 years. The Budds have pastored for a total of thirty-three years and have a rich experience in the things of the Spirit. They teach that believers owe the world an encounter with the living, loving God, and a gospel without power and love is not the gospel that Jesus preached.

The Budds founded and oversee the Firestorm School of Ministry, where believers learn to break off strongholds that hold back confidence, freedom, and anointing. Students learn to discern spirits, lead people in deliverance, heal the sick, and prophesy in the marketplace, at the workplace, and in the local church. Along with the local Firestorm School of Ministry, the Budds are also a part of a mobilized team of leaders who take the school of ministry to strategic cities and churches to train and equip leaders. The "International School of Ministry" (ILSOM) is a life changing experience and is an important part of the Budds' vision, especially for church pastors and their leadership teams.

Whether the Budds minister individually or together, the hallmark of their ministry includes physical and emotional healing and deep encounters with the Father's love and power. They partner with and minister in many other churches nationally and internationally who are also seeking authentic revival. This relationship network crosses denominational lines, helping emerging leaders walk together in purity of heart and the Father's love and power.

To contact Pastors Joel and Linda you may write:

Pastors Joel and Linda Budd
Open Bible Fellowship
1439 East 71st Street
Tulsa, OK 74136

or call:

918-492-5511

or e-mail:

lindab@obftulsa.org

Weekly sermons and teaching by
Pastors Joel and Linda are
available on the church website:

www.obftulsa.org

A Healing Week

Because of the many life-changing testimonies we are aware of, we strongly urge every individual and every couple of every age to experience a Healing Week through a ministry called "Restoring the Found-ations(RTF)." Dr. Chester and Betsy Kylstra have established a Healing House Network with trained, certified facilitators throughout the U.S., Canada and Europe.

As a part of the Healing House Network of RTF, we are also pleased to offer this ministry to you through several certified staff at Open Bible Fellowship. If you are interested in knowing more or in receiving a free brochure, please call the Healing Week Coordinator:

Healing Week Coordinator
Open Bible Fellowship
1439 East 71st Street
Tulsa, Oklahoma 74136
918-492-5511

Or E-mail your inquiry to:

info@obftulsa.org

Please include:

Name
Address
City State Zip Country
Phone
Fax
E-Mail

If the Tulsa location is not convenient for you, or if the waiting list is too long, we recommend you contact Restoring The Foundations ministry at:

www.RestoringTheFoundations.org

They have ministry teams and training centers in a number of locations throughout the world. They can also help to establish a Restoring The Foundations ministry program in your church.

If you are interested in the "Rite of Passage — No Regrets!" curriculum, please contact:

Pastor Cristin Hamman
Open Bible Fellowship
1439 East 71st Street
Tulsa, Oklahoma 74136

Or e-mail your inquiry to:

info@obftulsa.org

Other Materials From Pastors Joel and Linda Budd:

Fill Me or Kill Me

Are you desperate for more of God in your life?

Maybe you are crying out like Pastor Joel Budd did when he said, "Fill me or kill me, but don't leave me this way!" Or maybe you are ready to throw in the towel, as Pastor Linda Budd was, unless God moves in your life.

One thing is certain … you are on the right track because nothing much happens without a hunger and thirst for God!

That's why Pastors Joel and Linda have written their story. They tell how God answered them in a mighty way that transformed their lives forever and brought them into new dimensions of intimacy, revelation, and power in Him.

Their life-changing journey will challenge you to continue growing spiritually – because there's always more in the Lord!

No Longer Bound

Have you ever had your life turned upside down in the blink of an eye?

As 1985 turned to 1986, the lives of Pastors Joel and Linda Budd turned into a nightmare. When everyone else was celebrating the New Year, the unthinkable happened ... they learned that their precious four year-old daughter Joelle had been brutally raped. But this was just the beginning of the trauma.

Pastors Joel and Linda take you with them as they stumble through "the dark night of the soul" and finally experience God's tender and loving deliverance from the horrors of the past.

If you, or anyone you know, has been touched by violence, terror, or something unimaginable, healing and peace can be found! In the midst of life's most horrifying circumstances, God is there to deliver you. This is the remarkable story the Budds tell in No Longer Bound: A Story of the Father's Love.

And, Soon To Be Released...

Greater Is He!: Discerning and Defeating Destiny-Destroying Demons.

The wonderful truth is you have gifts, anointings and callings on your life from God. God has planted His grace and prophetic destiny in the very care of your being. You and your family line have generational blessings and divine destiny from God. That's the good news!

The bad news is that there are some very real and very negative forces at work behind the scenes that want to destroy destiny in our lives and our family line. At the same time, through unrecognized, unrepented generational iniquity, we can unwittingly open the door to help these destiny destroying forces gain ground.

The best news is that Jesus promised us that "Greater Is He!" This book may be the best news with the best results you have had in a long, long time in your walk with God. This book is co-authored by Dr. Chester & Betsy Kylstra and Pastors Joel & Linda Budd. As you read, you will be so encouraged at the effect on your mind, emotions and spirit. We are going to use God's authority to target the specific plans of the enemy against our destiny. You will quickly recognize some of the forces at work against your destiny or the destinies of your children and/or grandchildren.

You will be excited as you pray the anointed prayers in this book that specifically target some of the main "Destiny Destroying Demons." These unique prayers are being used by believers all over the earth with great results. As you see the increased freedom in your life you will likely hear yourself shout with joy and praise, "Greater Is He!"

"Through God we will do valiantly, for it is He who shall tread down our enemies" (Psalm 108:13).

More teaching series and resources are available from:

www.tlmtulsa.org

You may e-mail your inquiry to:

info@tlmtulsa.org